"Aim At Intact Work Groups.

The change strategy cascades throughout the organization embracing all employees and enabling intact work groups (i.e., boss-employee groups) to enhance their effectiveness.

Bottom Line: If culture doesn't change at the work-group level, it doesn't change."

"Avoid the Self-Managed Consensus Trap.

Encourage autonomy and clarity about authority. Without clear authority, there will be no autonomy. Decision effectiveness requires appropriate influence by knowledgeable and experienced employees as well as gutsy decision-making by bosses who know how to manage. Good sports coaches know this blend.

Bottom Line: You can have both—clarity about authority and appropriate, energizing autonomy."

"Whatever The Change Is, Don't Name It—Do It!

Naming it is to polarize opinions about it. "I'm for it." "I'm against it." For or against what? According to whose interpretation?

Effective change is integral to the organization's direction and makes it easier to succeed. Effective change is not something more to do. Rather, it is a way to do what is essential more effectively. It is not a burden. It lifts the burden.

Bottom Line: Do the change. Be it."

"Don't Confuse Training With Change.

Though organizational change may (and probably will) include training, that activity is a small part of success. Even then the training must not be packaged. It must be part of a strategy regarding who in the change process needs what particular training and when. Such training has to be sponsored by management—not HR, the Training Department, or Personnel.

Bottom Line: Think change, not training."

From Appendix A. Page 131

Other Business Books by Robert P. Crosby

Solving the Cross-Work Puzzle:
Succeeding in the Modern Organization

Walking the Empowerment Tightrope:
Balancing Management Authority and Employee Influence

Recent Book about Tuscany

A Month in Medieval Volpaia, Tuscany
Diary of a "Temporary Citizen"

Cultural Change in Organizations

A Guide to Leadership and Bottom-Line Results

Robert P Crosby

If you are interested in more information or would like to discuss the concepts presented in this book, please contact:

Crosby & Associates

West Coast:	206.369.9200
East Coast:	302.983.1429
or online at:	www.crosbyod.com

Book Layout and Design: Gayle Goldman Graphic Design
Cover Design: Norman Hathaway

ISBN: 978-0-9776900-3-9

Dedication

This book is dedicated to my Dad,

William Eli Crosby,

who would have been 100 years old in 1996.

Dad worked on the Pennsylvania Railroad and later the Monongahela Connecting Railroad of Jones and Laughlin Steel Company in Pittsburgh. He was a member of the United Steelworkers Union. He would never have dreamed that a book would be dedicated to him—a loyal, honest, productive hourly worker, and deeply spiritual person.

I'm sure Dad didn't think of himself as a leader. He didn't use the word. But he had a backbone of steel—his own personal authority. Given his spiritual depth, he probably would have preferred the humble phrase "servant leadership."

Perhaps that's the path one must traverse on the journey toward leadership, a path which transcends the old meanings attached to "authority" and the unrealistic fantasies associated with "consensus."

Cultural Change in Organizations

About The Author

On July 1, 2011, Bob Crosby celebrated his 83rd year. He's been around a lot of organizations in his time. A practical man, he has not always accepted the conventional wisdom about managing them.

When he began his working career, he was confronted by the negative excesses of the "everybody should decide" counter-culture of the 1960's. Bob first published an article about the critical importance of balance between authority and consensus in 1970. Since then he has been consumed with the need in both life and work for a balance which transcends these presumed polarities.

To the charge that he rejects the conventional wisdom advocating "participatory" or consensus-based management and "self-directed" or "autonomous" work teams, Bob says, "Not so. What people are reaching for in these approaches is absolutely critical to long-term organizational success. But there is no freedom without structure. Such movements become fads and fade away unless a balance is achieved between structure and involvement, between the leader's business objectives and employee initiative, between authority and consensus."

Cultural Change in Organizations tells how, in (mostly) story form, to create a culture that forges a powerful synthesis between management authority and employee participation and that therefore, leads to striking results in safety, quality, and productivity. It is written from Bob's extensive experience "in the trenches," that is, within organizations where he works on a regular basis with all employees—hourly to CEO. His work spans hi-tech, nuclear, government (city, county, and federal), manufacturing (union and non-union), the health industry, and non-profit organizations.

Bob founded the Leadership Institute of Seattle (LIOS) in 1969 which is now the LIOS Graduate College of Saybrook University.

His two previous business books are *Walking The Empowerment Tightrope: Balancing Management Authority and Employee Influence*[1], aimed at the manager/supervisor, and *Solving The Cross-Work Puzzle*[2] aimed at both working across departments in this cross-functional modern world and at Project Management.

Besides two Masters', Bob holds an L.H.D. (Doctor of Humane Letters) degree from Bastyr University in Seattle.

Finally, Bob has many hobbies and loves. His main two are singing and a daily ritual of roaming the corridors of Seattle's historic Pike Place Market. In fact, the first three chapters were written over a latte in a coffee shop there called SBC on the charming Post Alley. It could well be the fictitious "Castle Café" in the story. When not writing the author could be found, for nearly twenty years, singing in front of the original Starbucks with the legendary folk singer – the late – Jim Hinde.

Acknowledgments

Above everyone, the late Don Simonic looms! He was the Plant manager in Addy, Washington where my work in creating cultural change in organizations was solidified into the form that permeates this book.

Ironically, Don's first words to me were, "I hate consultants, but my boss told me I have to keep you!" Instead of reacting to the statement I found the simple honesty of it refreshing. Thus began a magic relationship. Don was an excellent sponsor (as defined throughout this book), colleague and, as we worked together, friend. He taught me as much or more than I taught him. For instance, it was his presentation at a company meeting that inspired me to develop the rainbow theory of goals on page 4 of this book.

In the next 6 years he took Addy from facing closure to a 72% increase in productivity, and rescued two other major Alcoa plants located in two different states (Tennessee and Indiana) while managing both at the same time. I'm told that in one of those years the two plants achieved over 1/4 of Alcoa's worldwide profits.

Don drove hard for results yet also recognized the need to nurture, support, and enable people to significantly influence their work.

In 1990 he urged me to create a special corporate graduate program to teach both management and hourly workers the skills of cultural change that we (Patricia and I) applied daily. The students were mostly Alcoans and included hourly workers from both union and non-union plants. Those who didn't qualify for the Master's Degree received College credits or, at least, a certificate. Over 400 completed the two year (12 weeks) program across the 15 years of its existence. Also, Don saw the importance of developing his top players. The fictitious "Luke" on page 33 is really Don, classic Don. That's how he recruited his own staff for the Graduate program.

Tom McCombs, a former student of mine, also deserves much credit. He brought me to Addy five months prior to

Don's arrival. Tom and I worked extremely well together: he as the Human Resource Director and I as an external consultant.

Special thanks to my wife and colleague Patricia, who was in the trenches of several companies with me and shared in the forging of Peter's strategy.

Currently my closest colleagues are my sons Gilmore and Chris. I am grateful to still be active with them.

I collaborated with Chris on this revision. In fact, without his urging, this book would not have been published. He inspired me to rewrite it, spent countless hours on it, and made significant contributions throughout. Special thanks go to him.

The stories in the book honor all the employees involved in our journeys and reflect a composite of real events. Many have told me that Peter's story is about them.

Those familiar with Edwin Friedman[3] will recognize his influence throughout the book which reflects the integration of family-systems theory with change theory.

Finally, why use the name Merlin? In one major change, workers and staff teased me about Camelot. Merlin books were circulated. Of course what I write here is "commonsense applied." There's no magic except in doing what is described here.

Decades later I've met many who describe those changes as special. Some were not sustained – that is disappointing. But others, who experienced the story written here that started with a plant manager who *hates consultants* and a consultant who knew how to not take it personally, went on to create their own "magical story."

Foreword

Cultural Change in Organizations
A Guide to Leadership and Bottom-Line Results

How can we best lead and create real cultural change? How do you help cultures move, such as those where people are overly compliant or where many employees seem hostile to leadership? (*See Appendix D for examples of cultural change.*) The answers to these dilemmas are here in this book.

In fact, the book is unique in that it was written after years of experience working in a variety of organizations and doing the tough work of cultural change. It is not primarily a theory piece, although there is some theory in it. My father, the author, was part of the first class in Organizational Development at Bethel, Maine in 1965. After that transformational experience: he went directly into organizations to hone his craft, rather than primarily into academia. This book distills his successful field experience in organizational development conceived as cultural change.

Thirteen years since its first publication, (originally entitled *The Authentic Leader*) the new title speaks to its real content. Prior to its new name, when I handed it to CEOs, business unit presidents, leaders, and other clients, I had to explain that it was about how to change their culture and achieve bottom line results.

Ironically, when first published in 1998, I took my first internal Organizational Development job at Alcoa Closure Systems International (CSI). At Alcoa CSI, I was blessed, but did not always find it easy during the first few years while finding my sea-legs. Although proud of some of my work– such as helping the Research and Design team launch new products–working in much of the organization was like pushing a large ball up a hill. In 2000 all that changed when a new manufacturing manager was hired for my region (North America). He knew how to execute and support the concepts in this book. He managed with clarity and purpose. By implementing these principles, I then enabled the two major plants to exceed their goals in all major manufacturing indices: Production, Scrap, Quality, On-time delivery, and Safety.

While reading this, if you find yourself saying "this cannot be done," you may want to refer to this foreword and remind yourself that it has indeed been done over and over again with our help in organizations in the U.S.A., Jamaica, Wales, Mexico and Italy. In fact, if you implement these principles in a methodical way, adjusted for your unique situation, you will reach your goals and have an engaged and committed workplace.

– Chris Crosby, President, Crosby & Associates West

About This Book

The philosophy that permeates this book is best expressed by W. Warner Burke's definition that, "...*organizational development is a process of fundamental change in an organization's culture*. By fundamental change, as opposed to fixing a problem or improving a procedure, I mean that some significant aspect of a culture will never be the same."[4]

While Cultural Change in Organizations is written mostly in story form, it is not fiction. Names are changed. Events are blended. Stories are embellished. But at its core, this book tells how significant cultural change leading to productivity gains have been made in real-world organizations and how you can achieve similar gains in a humane way for your organization.

At the heart of the successes that inspired this book are hourly employees. Thousands have been involved in the work described here. Hundreds have participated in the *ToughStuff*™ training described in Chapter 3. But more importantly they are leading in their day-to-day work situations. Certainly the word *leaders* in this book also refers to the CEO and those who are salaried employees. But more fundamentally it refers to anyone who dares to be authentic, to lead, to take a stand, and to interact in a non-blaming way. I have known countless numbers of hourly workers who are bringing such light into their organizations. My dad, a member of the United Steelworkers Union, would be proud.

What follows is a summary of the four parts of the book.

Part One: Peter's Story, which is based directly on my work with leaders of organizations, begins with Chapter 1. Peter is a CEO who is searching for a way to build and sustain a productive and humane organization. With the help of the wise and magical Art Merlin, Peter begins to learn about leadership. Peter's story continues through Chapter 3 and reappears in Chapter 6 and again briefly at the beginning of Chapter 7. But Chapters 1 through 3—which make up Part

One: Peter's Story—represent the heart of the book. Those readers who like stories best will probably start reading here. The other chapters in Part Two of the book are more didactic in nature.

In Chapter 2, Peter invents a process for organization renewal beginning with his own direct reports and searches for a balance which affirms his leadership authority while encouraging employee autonomy and participation.

Chapter 3 begins with Peter's visit to a high-performing crew in an industrial plant. Following his conversation with this group of unusual workers, Peter begins preparing a plan for intervening on the status quo in his own organization.

Part Two: Changing *Your* Organization is introduced by Chapter 4 which contains information and tools that you can use in *your* change efforts. The chapter begins by debunking self-managed work groups and, paradoxically, ends with a step-by-step guide toward the evolutionary development of greater autonomy in the workplace.

Chapter 5 continues the previous chapter's concerns by presenting an "action plan" for change. At the same time, I caution against a one-size-fits-all approach.

Chapter 6 describes a conflict resolution process which takes place in Peter's organization. Led by Merlin, this conversation between supervisor and employees is based on my experience with a manufacturing client where a long-simmering conflict had almost destroyed the effectiveness of a work unit. Doing this kind of work in an organization will be critical to Peter's eventual success. Woven into this chapter is helpful information about why and how Merlin, the facilitator, does what he does.

What is now Chapter 7 was written as a guide for managers planning structural change. Such change—the well-known corporate reorganization—is often intended to solve problems which cannot be solved effectively through structural change. Many attempts at "phantom" change actually serve to avoid real change and are negative in the long run.

Part Three of the book—A Theory of Leadership— is its most philosophical section. Chapter 8 is about authenticity—what it is, how we lose it, how we can recover it, how it relates to productivity in the workplace, and most importantly its role in leadership and cultural change.

In *Part Four*, Collected Short Stories, I return to stories from the organizations and people with whom I've worked over the past thirty years. I think of these stories as profiles in authenticity. The Short Stories record first-person accounts of events at the front-line of organization change. All are based on actual events in my consulting work with organizations, and their heroes and heroines have one thing in common: They modestly speak their truth. That is, they simply state their feelings, thoughts, hopes, fears, and goals while supportively enabling others to do the same. These are the stories of supervisors, hourly employees, an engineer, a clergyman, an executive, consultants, and a volunteer in a non-profit agency.

The appendices include a wealth of practical interventions that, by themselves, could transform the workplace if applied with skill. Also, these should be standard curriculum for Organizational Development programs. Such training must include both theory and supervised skill practice.

A few more words about Peter's story. Peter, in pursuit of his own blueprint for shifting to a productive culture, could be the owner or manager of his own 400 or 4000-person business or a department manager of hundreds in a mega-sized organization with many departments. Or he might be a "she" who is a small business owner with only 50-100 employees.

Art Merlin might be an internal specialist or external organizational consultant. Or perhaps he is simply that experienced, older, male or female employee/mentor who often surfaces at times of crises in successful organizations. Such people enable the emergence of authenticity because they themselves have wearied of the pretentious rat race and are most energized by truth. From such a stance, they exude authenticity and, thereby, encourage it in others.

Such people are clear about the proper relationship between authority and consensus in an organization and can demonstrate how authenticity bridges these two apparently divergent principles. They also know that authenticity leads to accurate data flow about schedules, commitments, what's working and what's not working, disagreements, and so forth. And, of course, all that translates into improved productivity.

Good reading!

Seattle, Washington, 2011

Table of Contents

PROLOGUE
Leadership and Culture

The use of too much authority or the absence of authority are equally disastrous.

The culture created by authoritarianism is well known. The culture encouraged by a vacuum of leadership is one of confusion, delay, and unproductive anxiety leading to increases in safety incidents, lower morale, higher turnover, and absenteeism.

Historically, the idea of the business owner as an authoritarian figure, dominating the lives and minds of his employees, ushered in the 20th Century. Later, the other extreme, popularly conceived as an authority-free style where all participants make decisions, was manifest in a variety of ways under names like consensus or participative management, servant leadership, 9/9 leadership, autonomous or self-managed teams. Both extremes fail. A management strategy which integrates these extremes is needed. The story that begins in Chapter 1 illustrates how any organization can find that elusive blend. The final chapter explains the role that authenticity—being who you are— and productivity—achieving the organization's goals—play in that intertwining.

The positive intent of authority, of course, is to get things done. The negative intent and frequent consequence is to run roughshod over people. The positive intent of consensus is to significantly involve people in decision-making. The negative intent and frequent consequence is to stifle action and give power to the most stubborn. The intertwining of the positives is a major theme of this book.

This revision keeps the emphasis of the original version that encourages clarity, straight talk, and firm leadership with maximum employee influence. That version as retained here was also a book about culture but perhaps more subtly put. For an example of an explicit reference to cultural shift see Appendix D. This simplifies the notion of culture and how one shifts to a more productive one without flags, whistles, or slogans. It may seem too simple but it works!

◆◆◆

Part One
Peter's Story

◆◆◆

CHAPTER 1

Peter's Dilemma:
How Do I Start a Cultural Change?

eter stood at his office window overlooking the bay. It
was a typical late fall morning in Seattle, gray and reflective. To a native like Peter, it was certain that the steely
mist would turn to rain by rush hour.

"Hmm, storm on the way out there, too" he reflected.
"And in here? Products are late, competitors are pricing lower.
And now there's this new employee survey data to deal with."

He turned toward his desk and, almost without thinking,
dialed a number. And as he replaced the receiver, Art Merlin
appeared at the door.

"What's up?" Merlin moved to the conference table where
they usually met.

"I'm frustrated and I need help. I hope your advice is as
magic as your name."

"You seem jumpy."

"Of course I am. We're losing market share, and now I
get this survey data from our workforce, and the news is not
good. Apparently, we're not seen as a make-it-happen company; quite the opposite, the employees think we'd rather
blame than fix. We have what the management gurus call a
'heavily blaming corporate culture.' The employees also say
that they can't count on their colleagues to come through
when they say they will. What's wrong with these people
anyway?"

"Nothing you couldn't change."

"Come on, Art, your gray hair doesn't give you the right
to blame *me*. See? There it is—that blaming thing. So, what's
your advice?"

"First," Merlin began, "you need to see the results of the employee survey as useful information.[5] Not definition. Not a list of things that are 'wrong with these people' or wrong with you. Then you need to take a few simple steps to—how shall I say—shift the thinking in your company. For example, it is possible within a few months to see a turn-around on this blaming business and major changes on the survey scores in all areas."

"You said 'a few simple steps.' Simple to whom?"

"Well, simple for me, certainly, because it's you, Peter, who has to do the work." Taking Peter's offer of a cup of tea, Art Merlin settled back in his chair. "Peter, you may call what I'm about to tell you 'common sense.' The difference lies between knowing it and doing it. Few do it. However, I've seen it done...several times. Now listen carefully. First you must accept that **you are the leader.** You've listened to your people. Now swing the bat.

"A wise man once wrote, 'Foresight is the *lead* that a leader has. Once leaders lose this lead and events start to force their hand, they are leaders in name only. They are not leading, but are reacting to current events....Foresight is the central ethic of leadership.'[6] Give up the illusion—the pretense—that your top management team will figure out where you should be headed. You've heard enough—you know enough to set a course. Now. Today."

Art moved to the white board and sketched three semi-circles.

FIGURE 1: RAINBOW MODEL OF GOALS

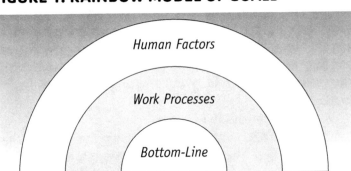

"The bottom circle signifies a *bottom-line goal*—a stretch goal to be achieved in the next six to 12 months. This could be a cost reduction or a significant growth goal."

Merlin was barely finished before Peter rushed to his desk and produced a thick document. "Look, here's our five-year strategy. We've already completed it and it hasn't helped!"

"A five-year plan? Peter, the Soviets tried that for half a century. No. I'm talking about a six-to 12-month goal that is at the core of your business success—or even survival."

"Well, we produce now at $3.78 a unit. Would a $3.00 goal be what you mean? Let's say by the end of the year—in nine months?"

Merlin eyed Peter for a moment. "Is it easy to reach that goal?"

"Not at all," responded Peter.

"Is it possible?"

Peter paused and then said, "Yes."

"Would it stretch your people?"

"Definitely."

"Is it critical? That is, can you help your employees anticipate their pain if you miss this goal—that's called 'delegating pain'?"

"Well, some will get laid off if we don't make it. You see, Merlin, at $3.00 a unit we will likely reverse our market share loss—that is, if we quit being so confounded late!"

Merlin returned to his diagram. "So, the bottom circle represents three bucks a unit achieved in nine months. Right? Now take the next semi-circle. Let it represent *work processes* that must be maximally effective for you to achieve the three-buck goal. You just said that some of your special projects are way behind schedule, and I'm sure your employees could name other processes and projects..."

Peter interrupted, "But they've done that already, Art. We have a list of key dysfunctional processes and little has changed!"

"Hold onto that despair for a bit, Peter, and focus on the top circle, the one that symbolizes how you are with people, *human factors*—the human dimension—how engaged people are in their work. For instance, are they focused only on task outcomes or technical knowledge and not on how processes work? And are some managers expert at 'shooting messengers,' which discourages work process improvements, while others are so permissive that there's no clear structure, no clear idea about who decides what?"

"Yes...all the above. In spite of training programs."

"O.K. Now I'll tell you what the best leaders do because I've seen them do it and do it with far more than the 400 people in your company."

Moving to the white board again, Merlin writes:

Rule #1: The leader leads.

"Like Columbus, the leader sets the course—the 'what' in each of your three circles—and stays the course in a non-reactive way against the inevitable resistance. You've heard them all before:

'It can't be done...'
'We tried this before...'
'All of us should decide...'
'I've got a better idea....' "

Writing on the board again, Merlin turns to another rule:

Rule #2: The leader communicates.

"I'd suggest this even if you had a cast of thousands. With 400 it's a piece of cake. Meet with all of your employees in groups of 20 to 50. Hey, this can actually work with several hundred at a time but keep it smaller if you can. Tell them what's up—the situation the company's in. Do it briefly. Tell them you're going to say more about your goals but stop at that point and receive comments."

"That doesn't work. I've asked for questions before and only two or three people talk."

"Great," says Merlin, "then don't do that again. Don't go down the same maze if there wasn't any cheese! Don't ask for questions—request comments. Don't worry about questions—they'll come. In fact, most of the comments will be phrased as questions. It's safer. People learn in their early years not to be authentic with authorities. One way we do that is by pretending our statement—our strongly held opinion—is merely a question. Don't fall for that. Begin modeling that it's O.K. to state a contrary point of view and that you don't have to hide it in this company! Be as concerned about communicating that value as you are about the content of the statements. Your company's future depends on it."

"I think I get what you're saying, Art. It's about data flowing honestly."

"Right. Accurate data flow, after all, is truthfulness, being authentic, saying what's so about goals, deadlines, differences, consequences, authority, decision-making and day-to-day work interactions. And it begins with you. It doesn't matter whether the 'data' deals with schedule commitment or technical opinions. Or feelings," Merlin suggested.

"Well, I don't really think the office is the place for that," Peter sputtered before Merlin interrupted him.

"Or feelings," Merlin repeated firmly. "Give me a break, Peter! Do you mean that no one has emotions at work? Feelings are simply another part of the data flow about what's actually going on. In most companies, information about feelings is routinely shoved under the rug, except maybe for anger or passivity which come out in blaming, and the result is that they run the show from there. Or rather run the meeting from under there! Better give them a place at the table, Peter.

"But back to your employee meeting. Before you take comments, have the participants talk in groups of two or three for about three minutes and discuss three things:

   ◆ What they especially agreed with that you said;
   ◆ What they are surprised or troubled about; and
   ◆ What was missing in what you said."

"They'll never do it, Art. Before I'm done giving instructions, there'll be five other suggestions about how to proceed.

In the past, I'd have tolerated no interference, which didn't work in the long run. Now that I've invited them to participate in really running the company, well, it seems like the lunatics have taken over the asylum. And giving orders is tough. I imagine they'll have at least 20 minutes of reasons why talking in small groups is a waste of time."

"And your response is 'No, I want it done this way,' and then you might repeat your instructions. Don't let the employees run your meeting. Give your instructions and turn away."

"So by doing that I'm demonstrating that I—not Mordred—am running the meeting."

"Mordred? Who's Mordred?"

"Well, you of all people should know that, Merlin!" Peter said laughing. "Mordred is my evil twin—you know, in the way that King Arthur and Mordred were enemies. He is the employee who blames someone else—often me—for every mistake, misstep, error, unintended consequence, glitch...for global warming and downtown traffic jams. Now that I think about it, the Mordreds—there are way more than one—are the source of the blaming culture in this company. He's everywhere, it seems."

"So he's running the company?"

"Well, some days it would seem so, Merlin. But it's not working, and I'm tired of it and am pretty angry at how I've let things get out of hand. Is he running the company? Well, not any more, he isn't," Peter concluded in a firm voice.

"Peter, in one morning's meeting not only will you demonstrate how to manage the Mordreds of the world, but also, by allowing the brief preparatory discussions, you will declare that everyone's voice is important. When time is up, ask for input from the back of the room, down front, everywhere. If Mordred speaks in a blaming way say something like, 'I get it, Mordred. You think it's my fault. And I accept some responsibility. Thanks for your comment.' Then look away from Mordred and say, 'Who's next?'

"Then it's time to share your goals—the three semi-circles. Be brief, clean and resolute. Have them partner again and give them another question:

♦ What's your piece of this pie, and what will you do to pull this off?"

"Delegate accountability," Peter says nodding. "But first I'll need to tell my direct reports and the union president. They have to own it."

"Of course, Peter, but be careful of the word 'own.' If you're going to guide this ship through the rough waters, your crew needs to be rowing in the same direction. Hear them. Hear their concerns. But you're not seeking a consensus or even a majority decision. The hard message is this—you won't make it with an unwilling or unskilled crew. You need to be as sure as you can that you have the right people, the right number of people, and the most streamlined organizational structure possible.[7] Peter, you need to be the beacon from which visions come and, above all, a leader who encourages people to unleash their own potential and ROW!" Merlin laughed.

Peter smiled. For a few minutes he stared out at the rain which had just begun to fall. "Art, I'm thinking of the story of the monkeys, where one monkey started washing the sand off yams with salt water, thereby making them palatable to eat. Then a second monkey started doing it, then another and another. By the time a certain number of monkeys—let's say a hundred—started washing the sand off the yams, then all the monkeys, even on other isolated islands, began doing the same. I believe in that 'critical mass' theory."

"I do, too, Peter, because I've experienced it. When you deliver your vision with simple clarity, your people will organize around that vision. Such leadership is so desperately needed and wanted. And as you model it, well, you just told about the hundredth monkey, so you understand."

"But there's more, isn't there, Art?"

"Yes, of course."

"I need a break to digest this. How about coffee in the morning at the Castle Cafe?"

By the time Peter left his office, a light rain covered the downtown area. Traffic barely moved but Peter had much to consider, so he was content at the slow pace. He was confused by some of Merlin's comments. "I have been a consensus leader," he thought, "and few will complain if I continue in this style, but just imagine the backfire if I step up to the plate and lead! Some will confuse strong leadership with a dictatorship. Still others think there are only two extremes on the authority continuum—either I decide or they decide—either authoritarianism or anarchy!

"Merlin is talking about a different way of doing things. But there's no question that the company's in trouble even though we have a good product and good customers. I'm the CEO, and I know that my management style isn't working. Of course, the problem could be global competition!" Peter smiled at this handy excuse so frequently cited in the 90's by CEO's of faltering companies.

"Well," he continued, "I can't eliminate global competition, but I can do something about how I lead my company." And with that, Peter felt better than he had all day. And as a new energy began to fill him, he declared, "This company's going to change, and it can rain until Christmas for all I care!" And, of course, it did. Change, that is.

CHAPTER 2

Peter Initiates A Process To Improve Each Intact Work Group

Merlin was already seated at his favorite table when Peter arrived at the Castle Cafe. Located in a midst of the busy Pike Place Market, all the energy and bustle of the city seemed to swirl around the tiny bistro. But its patrons felt temporarily cocooned in this clean, well-lighted place.

Settling in with their favorite lattes, Peter began the conversation. "I'm prepared to lead—with a clear vision—beginning now—staying the course and staying connected to my employees. And being authentic. Not just saying the right words, not faking it or pretending when I really don't know, but by being who I really am."

Merlin silently nodded his approval. These were important statements for the young CEO to make.

"I guess I'm a little embarrassed to admit that will be a challenge," Peter continued, "But I haven't felt this good in years. I'm feeling...I guess it's excitement. Or maybe I'm just scared!" Then, after a pause, "So, what's next?"

Lacking the white board, Merlin wrote the following on the nearest paper napkin:

Rule 3: The leader initiates a self-renewing process in all intact groups (boss and employees) and in cross-functional groups (projects and task forces where members report to different bosses).

Then he asked, "What does a 'renewal process' look like to you, Peter?"

Peter became reflective for a few moments and then began to speak about a special kind of gathering of his people. "I want to start with those who report directly to me...something simple...not rushed...no fancy charts, just a conversation about the important items:

- What's working well;
- What's not working well;
- What they need more of from me;
- Or less of;
- And what I need from them;
- What we are doing that we shouldn't;
- What we should be delegating that we're not;
- And the checks and balances that need to be in place for successful delegation."[8]

Peter's excitement becomes more evident. "Art, suppose I get my group together soon for a couple of days...and I'll present my goals!"

"Good approach, Peter. They'll be able to hear your vision, respond to it, identify their piece of the pie, and begin to strategize for immediate change. Until your group of direct-reports is aligned—headed in the same direction without covert or overt sabotage—nothing will change."

"You know," Peter scowled as he spoke, "Martha disagrees with me a lot. I've encouraged that in the name of openness, but now I need to take charge." Peter stops talking, then chuckles. "Either that or trade jobs with her. Art, I'm going to tell her that this is where I'm going, and I want her going down the same path. Further, I want her concerns turned into energy about how to overcome the obstacles she sees.

"So, Mr. Arthur Merlin, I may just borrow your first name for awhile. I'm ready to lead and I know where I'm going!"

Waving his empty cup in his hand, Merlin says, "Ah, you've found the grail, have you? Actually, you really needn't call yourself King Arthur. After all, Peter the Great and Peter 'the rock' were pretty good leaders themselves!"

Shortly, the two men took their departures, each regretting somewhat the need to leave this island of calm reflection. Lines from a Frost poem circulated through Peter's mind as he walked back to his office—"promises to keep...miles to go before I sleep." But rather than being burdened by such thoughts, Peter looked forward to meeting with his staff and starting this thing Merlin called the "renewal process." Peter preferred to think of it as, simply, effective leadership.

A week later, Peter boarded a flight returning him to Seattle from a brief business trip which he tagged onto the end of his two-day staff retreat. He hadn't yet had much time to reflect on its outcome. But as the aircraft climbed to cruising altitude, he settled into his seat and went over the events of the two days in his mind. Generally, he thought it had gone well. He became clear that, while the management staff had always felt respected by Peter, they hadn't believed they were truly being led by him. He reflected on an uncomfortable moment which had occurred early on the first day when Martha spoke up.

"It sounds unlike you, Peter, to be this assertive. In fact, you seem something like the old authoritarian you, and yet I know I feel safe speaking up like this—or am I?"

The group laughed nervously. Peter quickly responded.

"I really appreciate your asking that. You are certainly safe! I want different opinions expressed, but I'm no longer going to run this company by consensus."

"Then why should we express differing opinions? Either you decide or we all decide—you know that's the way it's been," Martha rebutted.

"That's a wonderful segue, Martha," remarked Merlin, whom Peter had engaged to assist at the retreat. "There is a Buddhist statement, 'Enlightenment is the path between the extremes.' It sounds like a hopeless paradox, but people can truly influence without consensus, and there can be clarity about who decides. There is no freedom without structure and clear decision-making authority. Peter has a critical role and others need authority to make decisions appropriate to their expertise and situation."

"Sounds heady to me," Tom interjected, "but I'm for it! I want clear goals, clear boundaries, and clear power to operate within those. I want to be able to challenge you when the goals or boundaries seem too confining, but darn it, when we can't agree, I want you, Peter, to take charge! I'll follow or I'll resign, but I won't sabotage."

Several of the managers became tense when Peter turned again to address Martha.

"There's something else I want to say that may seem harsh. It's safe to disagree, but it's *not* safe to be unsupportive of my decisions after we've aired our differences. I will not retain as part of the management team any key person who continually tries to change the course I set. I do not have time or energy for those who attempt to veto. That's the dilemma, the down side, to consensus. One person can hold out, can veto, veto, veto. In this group, we'll talk and if there's consensus—great! But we can't and won't talk forever!"

There was a long silence. Rather than feeling awkward as he might have in the past, Peter now felt confident that he had expressed himself with authenticity, manifest not in strident aggressiveness but in clear, compassionate, strong leadership. Art Merlin finally spoke up.

"Martha, Charlie, Tom, all of you. Is this a different Peter? And if so—a scarier one?"

"No," said Martha, "not scarier, but perhaps more formidable. I'm surprised at my response. I feel tense and yet relieved. Peter, you are already a great listener—sometimes you listen far too long. But I trust you as a leader. And I think we need a new kind of leadership now. I'm with you!"

Others chimed in in agreement. They were re-energized and ready to move forward with Peter.

As the plane made its approach to Seattle-Tacoma International Airport, Peter smiled to himself and thought, "They're ready to row, like Merlin predicted."

The following morning, Art Merlin appeared at Peter's office door. Peter turned from the window to greet him.

"The waters aren't as rough today, Art."

"I think you have a sturdy boat and a crew that's ready to row in the same direction, to continue the metaphor!"

"The two-day retreat gave us a good start, and now I'm setting up a series of communication sessions about my goals throughout the company. Also, my talk with the union president went well. He's concerned about the pressure of competitors on us. He not only wants to preserve jobs, but he believes the union ought to take the lead in creating a better work environment. Actually, he's ahead of me in some of this.... What's next?"

"Several things at roughly the same time," responded Merlin.

"Like on the napkin?"

Merlin and Peter laughed heartily when Peter pulled the wrinkled napkin from his coat pocket and spread it on the table. "I've completed this process with my direct reports, and now it's time to take the show on the road, right? I think I'll bring together the managers and supervisors and key salaried staff." Peter had clearly done a lot of thinking about his next steps. "We'll duplicate the retreat process I just completed with my direct reports with some key add-ons: We'll need to sort out who decides what and who does what and by when."

"That's important but it sounds like a new concern. What happened?" Art asked.

"I was talking last week to one of the guys on that high-performance team in manufacturing. I asked how they had increased their productivity so dramatically. He said that now they order their own parts and tools-—within limits, of course—and as a result have what they need within 24 hours. Before, the supervisor did the ordering with no promises about when the order would be placed or when the items might arrive. The workers simply had to wait until the stuff showed up. Having a retreat is one thing, Art; getting people to ask for and give 'by whens' across the organization is quite another! So, what I haven't figured out is how to move this across the organization—for instance, how to get everyone asking for and giving by-whens."

"Think of it this way," responded Merlin, "If the family is the primary unit in society, what are your primary units?"

"The crews. They produce the product!"

"So," Merlin continued, "the next step is to work with those crews and all boss-employee salaried groups, too. Help each of these intact groups to sort out:

+ What's working;
+ What's not working;
+ What the supervisor needs more or less of from her/ his direct reports;
+ What the direct reports need more or less of from their supervisor;
+ Which processes need to be re-examined and, if necessary, re-engineered by them; and
+ What needs to be delegated to reduce redundancy and dependency and increase effectiveness.

This way they can achieve their piece of the pie and keep track of who will be doing what and by when, while contributing their experience and expertise."

"That way they can learn it by doing it!" responded Peter. "And we could drive other things through the whole company by doing them—applying them during these intact group sessions—like clarity about who decides what!"[9]

"Yes, and at the upcoming retreat you can help each boss be clear about his/her unit's goals and..."

Peter interrupted, "Art, maybe it's time to have these groups become self-managed teams and eliminate bosses."

Suddenly Merlin vanishes. The chair he had been sitting in is empty.

"Arthur? Art? Gwen, have you seen Art Merlin?" Peter's administrative assistant's office was located so she surely would have seen him leave. "No, and I've been here for the last few minutes," she replied.

Both Peter and Gwen were puzzled and somewhat alarmed. Sensing this, Merlin spoke. "Sorry if I scared you. It's not something I can control. I just go FZZT and then I become invisible for a few moments when someone seems too excited and dogmatic about implementing self-managed teams or eliminating all bosses.[10] But if you mean that part of this work with each boss-employee group or with each crew will be to help them take their next evolutionary step towards less supervising and more autonomy, well, then, I'm totally with you. However, if you mean a radical move where all groups are now charged with managing themselves... well, then, FZZT I'm gone."

Peter was astonished. Not only had he never seen—or really not seen—someone become invisible, but Merlin's response helped him organize some of his previous random thinking about this issue and the reading he had done on it over the past decade:

- Managers flip from being authoritarian to being permissive and then back to authoritarian when permissiveness doesn't work.
- The history of management in the last half-century has been a swing from authoritarianism on one side to extremes of self-expression on the other as in the movements that emphasize consensus, self-direction, and empowerment with (sometimes) early honeymoon results...and then a swing back to the more predictable authoritarian style.

Then there was his favorite saying about parents that seemed to apply equally well to managers:

- Parents are authoritarian until they can't stand themselves, and then become permissive until they can't stand the kids.[11]

So, mused Peter, Merlin is talking about that path or balance between the extremes—how to move towards autonomy without throwing the baby out with the bath water—how to give clear leadership, steer the ship, be decisive, listen with empathy, stay connected, avoid the extremes. I need to see this with my own eyes—I need to visit a high-performing crew and hear from them firsthand.

> Good stories about the issues presented in this chapter are *The New Boss* and *Before And After...In A Non-Profit Agency* in Part Four: Collected Short Stories.

CHAPTER 3
Peter Plans His Change Strategy

A deep voice resounded against a backdrop of equipment noise.

"Hi, are you Peter Black? I'm Jim."

Peter nodded his head to Jim and looked around. He was on the production floor of a huge factory. He had visited this benchmark plant in the Midwest once before but had not walked through hardhat country. Looking around, Peter caught a glimpse of Merlin through an open doorway but as Peter moved toward him, Jim took Peter's arm and said, "Here, over here," and escorted Peter into a large room.

When Peter turned to wave Merlin over, he could see a few workers in the doorway but no Merlin. "Well," he thought, "This must be some variation on the disappearing act. He's disappeared himself and my office and landed me here, just where I wanted to be."

He turned to Jim and said, "Yes, I'm Peter Black. I wanted to visit a high-performing crew, an A+ group by all the best measurements—costs, quality and safety. That must be you."

Twelve men and two women were seated casually around the room. A guy in his mid-fifties spoke up.

"Who are you?"

"A fair question," responded Peter who spoke for several minutes about his role as CEO at another company and his desire to do things differently.

"Well," said a woman seated in the far left corner of the room, "I'll tell you there's been a big difference in the last eight months. They started respecting us. Before that they hired us from the neck down. Now they want our head— eyes, mouth, ears and brains, too!"

Peter barely knew what to say.

"Well, what do you do now that you didn't do then?"

A man to Peter's left, leaning his chair back against the wall, gave a boisterous, one-syllable response.

"Work!"

The room exploded in laughter. Speaking with a slow drawl a voice emerged from Peter's right.

"Well, I'll tell you. We always worked, but before the change eight months ago, we worked by order—sometimes at a snail's pace—and now we work at our pace...which is a hell of a lot faster. We don't have to do things twice or three times."

From each person— actually all twelve, Peter noticed— came stories of increased capacity to:

- Schedule work
- Order materials and tools
- Talk directly across departments rather than through supervisors
- Redesign work processes
- Manage costs
- Do safety investigations
- Solve problems on the spot

Peter was stunned at both what they were managing and at the unanimous participation in this conversation. Somehow he had expected two or three people to do all the talking. Peter wanted to ask about authority but didn't know how to phrase it.

"So," he simply asked, "What's Ann's role?"

"Ann who?" said one worker amidst what Peter took as good-humored laughter. The worker quickly said, "She's the difference. Since she became our supervisor eight months ago, everything's been different. She's a resource, a coach— and you better know this—she can be tough when she has to be!"

"Are you tough?" Peter asked as he turned to Ann.

"That's how I got the job. I'm seen as firm, I guess 'tough'—a woman who's going to succeed here has to be seen as tough."

"Yeah, but she's a softy, too," came another voice.

"So, do you call her 'the boss'?" responded Peter.

The question evoked a thoughtful response from several. They described her as a really good coach—the kind who tunes into people and will take a tough stand when necessary. They said that they avoid the word *boss* because of past bad experiences, but sure, she was the boss, a new kind who respected them. Someone said, "It doesn't matter if she's called boss, supervisor, or coordinator—like at one of the other companies in town—what matters is how she does her job. Everybody knows that she is accountable for her crews, and I know that I'm accountable for my part."

Peter had one more surprise. "Did you say 'crews'?" The answer was, "Yes. Three."

As quickly as he'd been transported to the plant floor, Peter found himself back in his office. "Didn't even click my heels," he mused, and as a bonus he was feeling no jet lag. He'd never thought much about magic and while Art Merlin's antics were surely dazzling, Peter was more impressed by the almost magical transformation he'd just heard about from the workers at the Midwestern plant. He leaned back in his desk chair and thought again about his strategy.

He knew not to take Merlin's ideas as prescriptive but rather as stimuli to his own creative thinking. He reflected on an old folk statement—"Our decisions make ourselves." Merlin had suggested that he not develop a slogan or use terms like "self-managed teams" for people to argue about and polarize around. Instead, he should honestly state the company's business situation, his goals, and help the organization (through the intact groups in the company) organize around that. In other words, he shouldn't implement a new program to bring about change but rather implement good management or, better still, effective leadership. What a simple, common-sense idea.

Knowing that other organizations following a similar strategy had achieved remarkable cost and people results, he filled a yellow legal pad with other steps that seemed critical to success. Expanding Merlin's three rules, he ended up with this strategy:

Peter's Plan: Steps 1–5

1. Set my goals and state them.
2. Help my direct reports align themselves with those goals. I tune in to them, hearing their concerns about how we get there, but I don't allow them to veto where I'm taking this organization. Our direction is not a consensus decision!
3. Meet with the union president and other union leaders as may seem wise at this point.
4. Communicate my goals across the plant in conversations with small groups. I'll talk about the big picture—the world scene, our competitors, about what we can control like safety, costs, and quality. I'll describe my bottom-line, work process, and human dimension goals and tell them that the ball is in our court. I won't let two or three negative, blaming persons dominate the conversation with employees.
5. Meet with my key salaried leadership, including the remaining first-line supervisors, to develop alignment on our direction and have each salaried person who leads an intact group sharpen his/her goals for the unit using the same three dimensions—bottom-line, work process and human factors.

Peter realized that Step 5 was critical because the real day-to-day "sustaining sponsor" of change in the organization wouldn't be himself but rather each and every employee and that employee's boss. The employees need to be self-motivated but led by their boss in a single direction.

Peter had heard of a company where, using video replay,

the leaders had individually practiced, in front of their peers, presenting the company's situation and their goals (their piece of the larger pie) to their direct reports. After feedback from the peer group (who took on the roles of direct reports) and a trainer, each leader had a chance to practice again until he/she was prepared to successfully communicate the company's situation—the big picture, the competitive factors, the goals for the unit—and engage in a lively dialog with the direct reports. The essential learning here was about how to lead without stifling dissent.

A really fine by-product of the process was the sharing of unit goals across units and the opportunity for the leadership group members to hear and support each other.

After this training, the next action—which really blew Peter's mind—was for each leader, cascading from the CEO on down, to actually make this presentation to his/her intact work group during the next few weeks. And, from what Peter learned, the process worked! So, it became his sixth step:

Step 6

6. Cascade conversations with intact groups throughout the organization including the leaders' communication of their goals (their unit's piece of the action); inquiries (assisted by a facilitator) about what's working/not working; and dialogues regarding clarity about by-whens, decision-making, roles, throughput, or whatever is blocking groups from being high-performing units.[12]

Especially in this step, Peter wants to make sure the boss-employee relationship shifts to a leader-leader relationship where everyone assumes leadership towards achieving goals. To help this happen, frank, open, reciprocal agreements need to be developed between the leader of the unit and the employees who increasingly see their own leadership possibilities as they get clearer about their own spheres of authority.

Peter had read a survey of six hundred companies indicating

that 30% of boss-employee work relationships were so sour that they needed to be addressed if meaningful, effective work was to follow.[13] Talking about goals or moving toward more autonomy seems fruitless if most of the employees' energy is drained by a poor work relationship with their supervisor. Probably only a skilled facilitator could help such a unit shift from a blaming to a make-it-happen stance. Conducting a "blame-the-boss" session with accusations and no reciprocal agreements from the unit members would only leave a bitter taste.

Worse yet, the company had gathered anonymous data in the past from bosses, peers, and employees and had fed this (usually accusatory) data back to bosses, hoping they would change. The assumption back then had been that people wouldn't be truthful unless the feedback was anonymous.[14] They didn't know that a skilled facilitator could make a big difference.

But a few months earlier, Peter had used Art Merlin in just such a capacity in a work unit that had been torn apart by a long-term boss-employee conflict.[15] So he was confident that he had competent help to assist work groups in resolving whatever relationship issues might be in the way of their moving forward. Also, as a part of this step, Peter wants each group to move in an evolutionary way towards less supervisory oversight and more individual autonomy.[16]

He realized that he was expecting a lot in Step 6 and that, as a result, each unit would need several additional, perhaps half-day, sessions following the initial one. Especially, he thought, units like purchasing, engineering, maintenance, and production might use this as an opportunity to improve their daily work processes as well as move toward more appropriate autonomy.

Peter also remembered his wife's story about the clinic where she worked. As a result of such sessions, significant changes were made to the charting processes, and the clinic was now handling more patients with less wasted patient and staff time.[17]

He could see that there must be constant supporting of individuals, groups, and managers/supervisors in informal "How's it going?" conversations. This was not a new program but merely good management. Training is on-the-job and continuous. In previous years, they had done a kind of team-building program and even had a follow-through session, but this was far deeper than that. If fundamental change is to happen, skilled change agents needed to be supporting productive work on a daily basis.

Breakdowns of agreements, work relationships, role understandings, and work processes are as inevitable as the breakdowns of equipment. The cynics say, "See, I told you it wouldn't last." The skilled manager knows that you can't wait two or three weeks for a follow-through session—for ongoing, informal, preventive (or reparative) maintenance— especially since many groups are coming from a troubled or, at least, a less-than-productive place. Imagine, thought Peter, if we tried to maintain or repair equipment the way we usually have (not) maintained work groups and processes!

With intact group work looming large in his strategy, Peter discovered a major grouping he had overlooked. Merlin had asked him when conversing about these steps, "Where's your biggest productivity possibility?" Without batting an eye Peter had responded, "The Century Project. It's our major new product, and it's already six months late!"

As he thought about that conversation, Peter recalled reading a recent book by a management guru which had highlighted the gradual evolution of cross-functional work since World War II. Peter realized how much he depended on projects that were developed by task groups where employees reported to many different bosses.

Walking down the hall looking for Merlin, Peter noticed him talking to, of all people, Mordred. He stopped some distance away but had no trouble overhearing the conversation which was becoming heated.

"Look, Mordred, there must be some mistake. You're arguing with me, but this is not my initiative. I'm a change agent for Joan, your boss. Tell her—not me."

Mordred turned away and quickly walked down the hall past Peter without acknowledging him.

Merlin called after Mordred. "I'll pave the way for you. I'll tell Joan that you'll be calling."

"Wow, Art, doesn't that put him on the spot?" Peter asked as he caught up to Merlin.

"No, he put himself on the spot. I issued fair warning yesterday that I would not listen to his complaints about Joan again unless he would use our conversation as preparation for his talking to her directly. I strongly believe gossiping is another form of sabotage, and I will not participate in it."[18]

Struck that clarity about boundaries was even important in a hallway conversation, Peter addressed Merlin about his new insight and concern.

"Art, I want to talk to you about cross-functional groups—especially the Century Project."

"Ah, Peter, it sounds like you are really getting serious. Cross-functional groups will make you or break you, but most companies seem blind about what to do. I want to show you something. Can we meet in a half-hour in your office?"

"Of course," Peter said, delighted that he could get Merlin's input. Peter was anxious to finish his plan, and the next step, Step 7, had to deal with cross-functional work groups.

Twenty-five minutes later, Merlin walked in and laid a diagram[19] in front of Peter:

"This is a graphic that helps predict how successful a task force or project team can be in its work. It basically deals with three questions:

- How skilled is the leader in interacting with others?
- How much clarity is there among the team members about the various task components?
- How healthy is the work system overall?

"If you can bring all three of these elements to a high level, then your Century Project will not lose any more ground and, I predict, will begin to gain on the schedule. I want you

FIGURE 2: THREE COMPONENTS OF A SUCCESSFUL ORGANIZATION

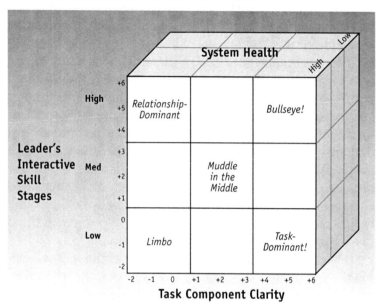

From *Solving the Cross-Work Puzzle: Succeeding in the Modern Organization* by the author

to know, Peter, that this model is based on practice—not abstract theory. And it works if you step up to your leadership role, your sponsorship role. Otherwise, forget it."

"So, I need to appoint good sponsors for my key projects ..."

"No," interrupted Merlin, "You don't *appoint* sponsors as I define that word. They already exist. Every boss is the sponsor of his direct reports and has authority to allocate their employees' time and resources. You appoint facilitators and project managers, and you assign single-point accountability, but you don't appoint sponsors. That is the most critical mistake made in projects. Rather than appoint, you identify who is the boss of every project member. That boss is already that person's sponsor and with a casual nod can discourage the project participant from cooperating in the task."

With emphasis, Peter interjects, "So, that's why the alignment of every boss who has someone on the project or task force is so critical. Boy, have I screwed this up in the past.

I've said to this or that person, 'You sponsor this,' but they haven't had legitimate authority to do so except with their own direct reports. (And even then it's not something you can *command*.) I've confused sponsorship with cheerleading or championing!"

"Merlin, that means that I, also, can't sponsor anyone except my own direct reports, right? No wonder I've failed on many organization-wide initiatives. I've given direct orders and passionate speeches on quality, empowerment and so forth but did not build alignment and clarity through real dialogue with those who manage and supervise the project participants. In one sense, I've led cheerleading sessions— rah, rah, let's do this—and people responded like they do to cheerleaders, but they went on about the daily business that they understood and were committed to! Worse yet, at times I've tried to institute new initiatives by E-mail."

"Exactly, Peter. Understanding *sponsor* as the way of locating the formal and legitimate power source rather than simply as a champion of a cause is the key element in assuring that the projects or products of task forces or committees are completed on time."

Merlin picked up a pencil and began to sketch on the yellow legal pad sitting on Peter's desk. "Draw a graph of who are the project members and then add their bosses names, and you will have the dynamic day-by-day sponsors who will make or break the project by how clear they are about the on-going priorities of their direct reports who are task force members. That clarity along with a decision-matrix are two key elements in project work when a task force is stuck on a critical, time-consuming decision. The decision-matrix will name the single person who will make the decision and end the deadlock.

So, Peter's seventh step took form.

Step 7

> 7. Work with the company's three most important cross-functional projects, beginning with the Century Project, to achieve task component clarity.

As Peter reflected on the Century Project he acknowledged that the Project Manager, Roberta, was highly skilled, both technically and in project management. But while her capacity to listen was not in question, she lacked the ability to take a stand and be decisive. Indeed, she had backed down at critical points and had gone to an "anyone-can-veto" style, even after decisions had supposedly been made. This stance allowed the schedule to slip by months.

On the other hand, Andrew, who managed one of the other projects, had a ramrodding, manipulative style. There was a small group who challenged him constantly and even larger numbers who talked behind his back and attempted to get him overruled. And a third group was not so overtly rebellious but found a number of opportunities to quietly be non-supportive of their project management and timetables. As Merlin described both the task and the interactive dimensions of his diagram, it struck Peter that many of his people lacked skills in change management, decisiveness, and the ability to listen. Reflecting on this with his direct reports, Peter created step eight.

Step 8

> 8. Develop a critical mass of employees who have system thinking awareness and high interactive skills - the capacity to take a stand, be decisive, stay the course against resistance, stay connected, focus on task component clarity, and improve system health.

Towards that end, Peter chose a training design with the following components:[20]

- *A one-day orientation.* Beginning with a statement by Peter about his goals, the orientation moves to a dialogue resulting in clearer identification by each participant about his or her piece of the pie. The success of this orientation is marked by decision-clarity and change-management clarity about how each will pull off his or her "piece."
- *A five-day training.* Experiential exercises in the context of work that challenge participants to:
  - Move from a stance of "victim" to that of "creator;"
  - Move from blaming to owning one's part in any transaction;
  - Move from arguing to having a dialogue (tuning in to the other);
  - Move towards integrating thinking with feeling and getting more in touch with one's emotionality, which influences all decisions;
  - Move from generalities to specifics and become more able to separate descriptions from interpretations about work processes and relationships;
  - Move towards speaking for oneself—saying "I" when "I" is accurate, "you" when "you" is accurate, and "we" when "we" is accurate;
  - Move from being inflexible and predictable in tense situations to having multiple options of how to be in those moments as well the ability to apply them;
  - Move towards being a leader who will take a stand and (a seeming paradox) listen more empathically; and
  - Learn key systems principles that apply to interpersonal communications, day to day tasks, and all changes big or small.
- *A three-day event.* This takes place about four to six weeks after the five-day training and is tailored to themes such as dealing with conflict, moving towards autonomy or whatever seems to be the relevant next step.

Here Peter remembered an earlier conversation with a department manager and his supervisors where Peter had encouraged them to think of themselves as coaches. To Peter's dismay and surprise, several supervisors had later reported that "...Having no authority just wasn't working." Peter was stunned!.

"They interpreted 'coach' to mean a loss of authority! I never met a coach without authority! Art, why is it that we always embrace the extremes. If someone says, 'be democratic' we interpret democracy to mean that everyone decides—the same with empowerment, employee involvement, and self-managed teams. Why does this happen?"

"Peter," Merlin had responded, "authority is a tough, emotional word with roots in one's early childhood. Adulthood is about finding my own authority while staying connected with my parents—not cutting-off from them, or continuing an adolescent rebellion, or a placating fusion where I continue to say what I imagine they will approve of. When people haven't worked out these fundamental authority issues with parents, they will crop up again and again whenever they have a teacher, a boss, or even when they themselves are in authority. Since most folks haven't resolved this aspect of adulthood, they think in extremes about authority wherever they meet it—or they deny the need for it and pretend that all people are at the same level."

"I'm embarrassed when I think about this, Art, but I've done just that. I've managed this company in a denial about authority. I've pretended that we all were deciding—I would even say 'Let's decide' when really I was deciding. Then I'd feel guilty. But on the other hand, Art, we can't do therapy for everybody."

"Of course not, Peter. They don't need therapy. They need clarity. You must lead and train for clarity. The authority issues are bound to come up—in the company and in the training. Don't ignore them. Face them. Without clarity about authority you will not succeed in your quest. Everyone must assume his or her own appropriate authority! Think of it this way: *Authority is*. It is neither good nor bad, but it can lead to positive or negative results. You cannot eliminate authority. It will always arise. Whether it's gangs in the city, so-called 'self-managing' teams where supervisors are eliminated, or twenty people stranded on a deserted island, authority will always arise. Sometimes the results will be positive, sometimes negative. You, Peter, cannot afford to leave that to chance."

With that, Peter designed the fourth component of his interactive skills training:

+ *A coaching follow-through.* This second three-day follow-up session would further sharpen skills not covered in the first follow-through and train each participant to take a third-party role, helping two other parties iron out obstructive work relationship dilemmas.[21] It would develop both the managers' and the supervisors' capacities to tune in to employees and to appropriately set goals and expectations, monitor work, and do consequence management (reward or punish). This work would emphasize both dimensions—tuning in as well as personal authority/authenticity. Hourly workers in the training would also gain skills in conflict management and in constructive ways to engage peers and bosses in dialogue about possibilities and concerns.

Early the next morning, Peter spotted Merlin at the Castle Cafe, his head buried in the morning newspaper.

"You're unpredictable, Art, except for one thing...I can always find you here at this hour."

"This is definitely an important ritual for me. Let me get you a cup of coffee."

Settling in, Peter showed Merlin his notes and began talking about his eight steps.

"I love your excitement, Peter...and your approach. But beware of 'steps.' Keep them dynamic! Don't publish them! Use them as your guide but know that you may shift the order or change the direction. *Stay firm about your goals but flexible about your process.*"

Merlin let his admonition sink in for a minute and then continued. "A question—how do you choose who comes to the training sequence?"

"Late yesterday, I had a fascinating conversation with Luke, the CEO you referred me to," Peter replied. "He blew my mind! He told me to ask my direct reports to list, including themselves, who we could *not* afford to have off the floor for extended training. Then he surprised me by saying that those listed should become our attendees! He emphasized that this is an investment in my strategic success, and I need my key people there![22]

"It's an *investment*, Art, not a training! He further suggested that I select key people—a vertical slice of my company from a couple of direct reports and supervisors to staff and hourly workers—and train them with advanced skills in conflict management, cross-functional processes, meeting facilitation, intact work-group continuous improvement sessions, and so forth. In other words, I should develop a cadre which will help sustain the shift in culture and the alignment around my goals."

"So you have a ninth step."

"Yes, thanks to you and Luke."

Step 9

9. Appoint a cadre of key people early in the process so they can engage in all of the steps. The cadre will have two roles—observing and evaluating our change process as it plays out in their own intact work group while simultaneously being participants in the process.

"Peter, you're on a roll."

"Yes, and speaking of shifting a culture, you're quite a change agent yourself, Mr. Merlin. Above all, you've helped me believe that I can achieve a cultural shift and get significant productivity gains sooner than I had imagined. But not if I try to use a cookie cutter and force every intact group and every work crew into becoming exactly the same. And most important of all, the key is in sustaining the change because change never ends!"

Preparing to leave, Art began to stand up from the table only to feel Peter's hand on his arm, urging him to sit a while longer.

"I want to understand the FZZT thing. Can you give me some of your magic?" Peter was only half joking.

"Peter, there's no magic."

"But you became invisible!"

"I didn't do that—you did. You, in that moment, lost the path between the extremes and needed to experience a work crew where authority and employee involvement are balanced. When you suggested we throw our managers overboard you went for a quick fix—a radical concept of team functioning you wanted to impose on every group without clarity about authority. Do that again and 'poof'—*you* will be invisible and so will all your change agents and all who would otherwise self-organize around your goals."

After a moment of silence Peter looked at Merlin.

"OK, I get it. I hold the magic in my hands. My job is to create a culture, a context, within which people can grow and contribute. When I lead, I model leadership for everyone, and then we can all unleash our own magic."

Merlin, who had been leaning forward attentively, slowly sat back in his chair and then said, "But, of course, sometimes the genie stays in the bottle."

"Well, Merlin," Peter replied, "Life is unpredictable. But, then, it wouldn't be very exciting if we knew, for sure, the outcome."

The two men grinned at each other and ordered another round of lattes as Merlin said, "And how about those Mariners...!"

For more stories, turn to Chapter Six and follow Merlin as he deals with a tough conflict between a boss and subordinates. For project/product management see Appendices M and N. For a short version of Peter's Change Strategy, see Appendix B.

Merlin's Secret

If there's magic,
If there's a secret,
It's that *leadership* is not about charisma.
It's not about hyping people.

It *is* about clarity.
If the head leads, the body will follow.
If the leader is clear—
Stays the course,
Stays in touch—
People will choose to come along
With their own clarity
About their own piece of the pie,
Their own part in the dance.

◆◆◆

Part Two
Changing Your Organization

◆◆◆

CHAPTER 4
Autonomy and Productivity

I n the 1970's, a revolutionary event occurred in U.S. business. A new industrial plant opened, introducing autonomous or self-directed work teams, that is, teams with no formally-assigned supervisor. While other organizations had attempted such work groups, no heavy industry plant had ever begun its life in this way. Like the Uddevalla Volvo plant in Sweden (which eliminated foremen in the 1980's), the Aluminum Company of America's (ALCOA) magnesium plant was heralded as the "wave of the future." Visitors, intrigued by the concept, flocked to both plants.

The Uddevalla plant closed in 1992. Critics say the organizational structure fostered a management philosophy that was more like abandonment than empowerment. Proponents emphasize the humanistic environment and gradually-improving productivity as unacknowledged signs of success. Nevertheless, the plant had not achieved competitiveness with other Volvo plants or foreign competitors.[23]

The ALCOA plant, though in serious trouble in 1990, was hailed in mid-1993 for boosting productivity by 72%.[24] In November, 1992, *Metals Week* called this plant the "only ray of hope for U.S. customers."[25] The article cites ALCOA's "ground breaking productivity" as an example of this success.

While the story of the Uddevalla plant has been described thoroughly,[26] the remarkable turnaround at the ALCOA plant remains either untold or, worse yet, the increased productivity is ascribed to the emphasis on self-directed teams or a more effective use of technology. This is how myths become truths and blur reality, or at least my version of reality. I say this because my colleague (and wife) Patricia Crosby and I were called in as consultants to this plant and helped ALCOA with an intensive change process that lasted two-plus years.

Abdication of leadership/responsibility was evident at the plant when we arrived in late 1989. Decision-making by consensus was rampant, and almost everyone had the ability to veto or at least slow down decision processes.

The dominant social style of eighty percent of the employees valued amiability, expressiveness, and spontaneity. The culture rewarded these traits so strongly that no one among the management had a style that emphasized a primary concern for bottom-line results! That is, until Don Simonic arrived as plant manager in mid-1990. His ability as a leader together with his capacity to

- Be truthful;
- Set breakthrough goals;
- Connect with employees; and
- Develop clarity about authority throughout the system

was essential to the plant's turnaround. And he exposed the myths about self-directed groups! Terms such as "self-managed," "self-directed," or "autonomous work teams" typically refer to work teams with no foreman, supervisor or manager who is held accountable for the teams' functioning. But whoever creates a team can *un*-create the team; whoever creates the team is, thus, accountable. In addition, there is rarely a team with no leader. Organizations—like Nature—abhor a vacuum, particularly in leadership. So, someone fills this void, however indirectly or ineffectively.

The primary task Simonic faced was to get authority—especially in the supervisory ranks—clarified and in place in the system. Where the role and authority of the supervisor aren't clear, the authority of the worker is also confused. In such a vacuum, a few workers will often take over and become the new authorities, for good or ill. Likewise, staff authority becomes confused. If line managers don't seize the reins of responsibility, staff and/or employees will understandably step in to fill that authority vacuum. Although this could be seen as helpful in short-term, emergent situations, it will be confusing to all and detrimental to the system if it continues.

The psychological function of leadership is to define limits and, in doing so, create enough structure for employees to feel safe. This is why leaders always emerge where there is an authority vacuum, whether it be among youth in the city streets, nations that are floundering, or a work group that is told to "do it yourself" without the necessary clarity about authority. In such a quagmire, a manager will usually micro-manage the crises and generally abdicate during non-crisis times.

In our consultation process at the plant, Patricia and I teamed with two key internal persons: sponsor and leader Simonic and human resources manager Tom McCombs who had a 15-year history at the plant. Simonic, in his role as plant manager, exhibited strong leadership. That is, he was clear about

- Where he was going ("We're going to reduce costs per pound by 20% in one year and work <u>with</u> people in the way all of us want to be treated");
- How they would get there (by involving people in improving processes and working together); and
- The need to be connected with his employees while staying the course against resistance.[27]

In short, he was willing and able to take charge *and* tune in to his employees.

No organization can for long allow a team to function with poor productivity or quality, unsafe work practices, or high absenteeism. Yet, such supervisor-less groups may continue functioning ineffectively for years while management frantically tries indirect ways to influence their performance. One such indirect way is to change personnel in the groups. Usually, however, once a negative work culture develops, the new personnel coming onto the scene get sucked into the old negative culture unless they are unusually clear about their own personal authority and will stand up against work norms that discourage eagerness or diligence about work.

Effective management, operating out of a humanistic set of values, is an appropriate blend of the head (thinking, including the transmission of information and the capacity to listen), the heart (values), the gut (the honoring of one's emotions and intuition), and the backbone (the willingness to take a stand against resistance). Situations like the one described above develop because one part of the system is out of kilter—too much heart, too little head and no backbone, perhaps. However, an organization where head and backbone run the show may be a dreary, if not intolerable, place to work. A major goal at the ALCOA plant was to assist crews to move from a permissive, consensual, idealistic, and unproductive model to a productive one that balanced management authority and worker influence.[28]

Clarity About So-Called Self-Managed Teams[29]

"Self-managed" means different things to different people. Think of it this way: *A self-managing unit manages what it manages and doesn't manage what it doesn't manage.* Sound crazy? Stay with me and consider this example and the diagram in Figure 3.

Suppose a unit is expected to manage the following items:

- ◆ Safety
- ◆ Productivity
- ◆ Quality
- ◆ Environmental impact
- ◆ Its own meetings effectively
- ◆ Discipline of employee tardiness, absenteeism, rule violations

If there are four units, will *all* of the units manage *all* of the items well? Of course not. It is likely that the time-honored, bell-shaped curve will be in force here as it is in traditionally-managed units. (Notice that I've switched my reference from teams to units. Team implies working together, "teaming." Some units don't need "teaming" but do need more individual freedom. For instance, maintenance employees may work in pairs but rarely as a team. Social service personnel often need to be freed from team obligations to do individual work. The question is: How does the unit need to be organized in order to function productively? Certainly, the answer is not always "teaming").

FIGURE 3: NORMAL DISTRIBUTION

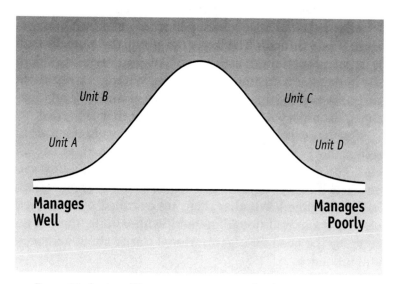

Even Unit A will not manage perfectly. So, who manages when the employees are not managing well? This is the question that *must* be addressed. It is a fundamental issue of modern organizations—*finding the proper balance between management authority and employee influence* and helping the supervisor develop the art of intervening when needed while avoiding micro-management.

Supervisors (call them what you please—it doesn't matter) and the managers above them have single-point accountability, and their goal is to create increasingly more autonomy until employees are able to function like Unit A in the bell-shaped curve. When the unit is not functioning in a high-performing way, the supervisor has single-point accountability to step in and say, "I need this to be handled by (a certain time). If not, I'll manage it."

Thus, each unit defines the degree to which it is supervised by the effectiveness of its own self-management. In essence, the supervisor's offer to the unit is, "If you manage the work process effectively, I won't need to manage you." *But don't expect a supervisor to achieve this with hourly employees if the supervisor is being micro-managed from above and is not experiencing appropriate delegation!*

After an initial honeymoon period, so-called self-management is very difficult. The larger the group, the more difficult it is. Many such units look more like group tyrannies than the honeymoon dreams of consensus. Without clarity about authority and continuous maintenance of work role relationships, the units will fail—no matter what they are called.

One important concept that often gets lost in the rush to restructure is this: Self-managed units are a method, not an end. The end is to achieve the organization's mission, values, and business objectives. The end is not to create *teams*, however defined. Whether there are so-called self-managed units or more traditional foreman/worker units, there is no escaping the need for organizational clarity about authority and influence.

In real life we citizens of a democracy manage ourselves but only within the framework of law and societal and organizational expectations that our body politic has created. In a similar manner, work units develop norms or "ways to work—or avoid work." If the norms are unproductive someone must have the authority to intervene before the organization faces a business crisis. If organizations are to flourish, we must stop thinking of authority in pejorative terms and dismissing its reality. Authority is not bad or good—it simply is. It can be used for good or ill. Pretending that it does not exist is the kiss of death; sharing it, with balance, is empowering to all—bosses and employees.

Authority best applied is what I call "leadership," and at ALCOA leadership was the key element of the change strategy we followed. But what traits should we look for as predictors of effective leadership? It may seem obvious and redundant to say that the CEO, managers, and supervisors must lead. But, in reality, many frequently don't. You have already read here that a leader must provide a clear authority structure while staying genuinely open to employee influence. Leaders must avoid the extremes of dictatorship or abdication. As Peter discovered in Chapter 1, the early phase of a change process includes strategies where the key leader meets for dialogue in small groups with employees organization-wide. "Here's where I'm taking the plant. I'm eager to hear your reaction. I'm enlisting you to help me pull this thing off."

The following questions are critical for any unit:

1. What is the authority structure that guides the unit?
   - The formal authority structure set up by the organization
   - The informal structure within the group, i.e., the way it really works
2. What are the gaps in practice between the formal and the informal authority structures?
3. What is working well in the authority structure? What is not working well? What needs to be changed in the formal document or in the informal practices to achieve high performance?

And what, in some organizations, makes it important at times to perpetuate the fantasy of consensus by using jargon such as self-managed, self-directed, or autonomous teams?

Warren Bennis writes about the "unconscious conspiracy that prevents leaders from taking charge." He goes on to say,

"When everyone is his or her own boss, no one is in charge, and chaos takes over. Leaders are needed to restore order, by which I mean not obedience but progress."[30] Referencing the assassinations of John Kennedy, Robert Kennedy, and Martin Luther King in the 1960's, he writes, "We lost our leaders, found no one to replace them, and decided to do it ourselves."

And as part of this same shift in Western culture, not coincidentally, the plant at Uddevalla is born, and as the last decade of the 20th Century plays out, America's long-standing ambivalence toward strong leaders reaches from the Presidency to the family and deeply into the work place. To lead means to "stay the course" in the face of resistance to change. Many give up, go to consensus or authoritarian extremes, and hope for the best.

Organizations live in much pretense about authority. Managers say "We will decide," when they mean, "We will decide unless I don't like that decision. Then I will decide." Such pretense is destructive and disempowering in the workplace. Just as children are not able to grow in a healthy way without clarity about structure and authority, so work crews are not able to perform effectively or be appropriately empowered if they are unclear about who truly has authority to do what and decide what and if capricious decisions are made, without consultation, about issues, resources, placement, equipment, materials, processes or schedules in areas where they work daily and therefore probably have the greatest knowledge. Also, fear of unjust authority often results in rule by the most threatening member of the group or no clarity about authority at all. Both extremes are equally disastrous.

The struggle to find an effective model for managing is not unlike the 20th Century struggle in education. Most traditional education was authoritarian and focused on the transmission of information. Using the analogy of the body, the "head" was dominant. The teacher passed on information to the pupil as well as the correct interpretation of that information. Then along came "progressive" education as a direct reaction to the authoritarian model. In its extreme, pupils could choose their own individual pursuit in the classroom with little or no guidance. The "gut," not the "head," was dominant.

John Dewey stood in the middle, criticizing traditional education for its fixation on authoritarianism and its inference that learning is merely the transmission of ideas and, at the same time, chiding progressive education for its over-emphasis on freedom. Writing in the early part of the century, he warned that there is no freedom without structure.[31] Without knowing about Dewey or his philosophy, the most productive organizations have found the right balance between freedom and authority without making a sham of freedom or becoming tyrannical.

The act of creating that balance is *delegation*. Most employees want some say in the design of work processes and procedures, in general resource allocation and procurement, and in measures that affect the safety of their work place. But first they want clarity about assignments—who does what and who decides what.[32] These are the questions that must be answered to give them that clarity:

1. What is currently decided by the boss with little or no input, what is decided by the boss only after consultation, and what decisions are delegated?
2. What changes in the above decision-making patterns are desirable within the next three, six and twelve months?
3. What training, coaching, or information will be needed to support such a change?

In an authoritarian environment, the answers to "Who decides?" is "the Boss." However, if the organization embraces autonomy, the answers to the above questions can help move each group on its own path and, therefore, the organization toward more humane and more productive goals .

The movement toward a more humane and productive organization is a movement toward employee autonomy. And to many employees, "autonomous teams" sounds like the un-managed, confused teams many have experienced in organizations. This interpretation will simply bring added confusion about authority. So rather than talk about this issue directly with grand announcements about moving the organization in one direction or another, the leader needs to let the meaning of autonomy become clear in the doing of it—by modeling it, by delegating, by "walking the talk."

This is how Howard did it. On his first day as supervisor of a crew, he received a couple dozen phone calls from crew members requesting that he call someone, frequently to order materials. In each case, Howard said, "I'd like you to go ahead and place the call yourself. That way you will be sure your request is recorded correctly and, when appropriate, you can get specific commitments about delivery date and pricing." He repeated this response every day for two weeks, until the calls quit coming in. When he followed up with crew members, they were enthusiastic about the increased control they now had over their work processes, both in quality and productivity. They were now making the contacts that they were perfectly capable of making.

Howard avoided the kind of employee resistance that meets leaders' announcements of a "new program of self-managed, autonomous teams." New programs are not what's needed; rather, people need clarity about authority, responsibility, and opportunity.[33]

Employees are not empowered by self-directed fads that ignore decision clarity. Most empowerment and autonomy-oriented programs leave them feeling *dis*empowered and betrayed, much the same way that old style authoritarian leadership does. Employees know a lot about productivity and want to contribute positively at work. They expect their leaders to lead. They will resist change (don't we all?) but they are ready to follow a leader who will tune in to them—take a stand—tune in to them—take a stand—tune in.... Such leadership transcends the imagined polarities that have plagued us in this century.

Returning to question 2. about the speed—three, six, twelve months—at which changes in decision-making authority will occur, it is important to recognize the essentially evolutionary nature by which (relatively) orderly and effective shifts in the balance between management authority and employee influence take place in an organization. A sudden, revolutionary switch in a more traditionally managed company to "self-managed, autonomous work teams," like moving directly from Profile 1 to Profile 4 in Figure 4, is dangerous and likely to fail: To many employees and supervisors, it simply means that the boss no longer has authority and the workers are in charge. The baby's thrown out with the bath water.

This need not happen. The movement toward more autonomy for salaried and hourly workers in an organization need not be chaotic or counterproductive. A plan for such a shift is presented in Chapter 5. It is based on the following principles. But here's the caution: Whenever you begin to sound like you have a program, abandon your plan, at least temporarily, and retreat into these principles regarding change:

Principle #1. Authority can not be eliminated.

It always exists. It exists even if people pretend it doesn't. A gang of teens will always raise up someone to the authority of the gang leader. A "self-managed" unit will do the same—sometimes with positive results but often with negative results over time. Answers to questions like who's in charge, who decides what, who measures whom against what expectations define the parameters of a formal authority structure.

FIGURE 4: STAGES OF AUTONOMY

Profile 1	Profile 2	Profile 3	Profile 4
Safety	*Safety*	*Safety*	*Safety*
Doing assigned work	Doing assigned work	Doing assigned work	Doing assigned work
	Some decisions about work	More decisions about work	Decisions about work
	Costs	Costs	Costs
Orders materials	Production output	Quality	Quality
Monitor above		Coordinate work	Coordinate work
Control as needed		Production output	Production output
Coach as needed		Order materials	Order materials
Discipline	Order materials	Safety investigations	Safety investigations
Absenteeism	Monitor above		Recommendations about discipline
Costs	Control as needed		Absenteeism
Decisions about work	Coach as needed		Vacations
Safety investigations	Discipline	Monitor above	Overtime
Quality	Absenteeism	Control as needed	Discipline
Coordinate work	Safety investigations	Coach as needed	
Production output	Quality	Discipline	
Vacations	Coordinate work	Absenteeism	Monitor above
Overtime	Vacations	Vacations	Control as needed
	Overtime	Overtime	Coach as needed

Supervisor Tasks (lower-left) — *Employee Tasks* (upper-right)

When these parameters are missing, an informal authority structure will emerge. In the long run, most of the various informal structures—if they prevail—will prove wasteful, unable to handle conflict effectively, and unproductive in achieving the company's objectives.

Principle #2. Movement towards autonomy is what effective leadership is all about.

As I indicate earlier, leadership is not a program with a catchy name! The process outlined in the next chapter is simply effective management or, rather, effective leadership. It is as natural as the flow of water. With encouragement it can evolve in accelerated ways, just as water will flow faster if impediments are removed from the stream. If you name it, you polarize it. People will be for or against any perceived radical change. Go with the flow and accelerate it where you can.

Principle #3. Be careful what you ask for.

While movement from traditional to non-traditional is generally wise, it is not always so. In the graph shown in Figure 5 there is a correlation between movement to the right and improvement in costs, safety, and quality.

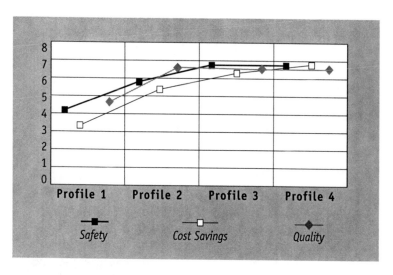

FIGURE 5: RATING OF WORK GROUPS BY SUPERVISORS

This data comes from a study where supervisors first chose the profile that most matched their work unit and then rated their profiles on a eight-point scale for safety, costs, and quality derived from hard data. Eight represents a perfect performance, zero the opposite. Over 150 supervisors and groups are represented in the data presented in Figure 5.

So if movement to the right on the graph in Figure 5 is generally associated with better performance, shouldn't every smart manager institute a Profile 4 structure immediately? No! What if you have a Profile 1 unit that scores "world class" in safety, costs, and quality—a unit whose members feel respected by their boss, from whom they want an orderly, stable work place? Despite the general trend noted above, some Profile 1 groups score quite high—think of great sports teams, for example. In short, if it ain't broke (you know the rest).

In addition, without careful attention to the checks and balances outlined later in this chapter, it is common for units attempting radical change to end up at "Profile 5": No apparent direction, no accountable management, and no clarity about who does what or decides what, a permissive style that is off the chart.

Principle #4. Don't move every unit at the same speed or expect every group to look the same.

Beyond the caution not to move radically, it is important to acknowledge the particular nature of each unit and make its shift toward greater employee influence a unique product of the unit's own special character. This is why programs often fail—when they are applied as inflexible templates for all occasions, denying the special way in which we each view ourselves. People and organizations don't respond well to straight-jacketing!

Principle #5. Be wary of the word team.

Think of it this way. Are your direct reports or crews really a team like, for instance, a sports team? As indicated earlier, members of the typical maintenance crew often work individually or in pairs spread throughout a plant. In what way are they a team? Why not think of them as employees who have some things in common, who need to collaborate occasionally, but who really need to be free to function independently rather than become a team? Look at any group of employees (salaried or hourly or volunteers in an agency) and ask, "What does each person need to succeed, and how can those in charge provide leadership to pave the way for success?" If teaming is crucial, then create an effective team. If not, don't. "Team" is a method, not an end!

Principle #6. Encourage the movement toward more autonomy within a larger strategy.

Peter's story is a good example. Simply moving towards autonomy without a larger context and strategy and without making tough leadership decisions (for instance about having the right people, the right number, in the right places) will relegate the movement towards autonomy to a program status—another program-of-the-month which will not be sustained. The movement toward employee influence and autonomy are big ideas, but they must rest within an even larger picture, that is, they must serve concrete business objectives.

A good story about the issues presented in this chapter is *Besting The Best* in Part Four: Collected Short Stories.

CHAPTER 5

How to Move Toward
Increased Employee Autonomy

ABOUT PLANNING

I have cautioned against instituting a *program* of change and yet it is important to plan and guide the change process carefully. The plan outlined below is just that, a plan. It is not a one-size-fits-all prescription for managers or an all-purpose program to fix an organization. But, having said that, is it possible to plan change at all?

Yes, if we return to our notions about leadership and authenticity. Leadership is the key ingredient in the process. To the extent that the leader stays in touch with his/her guts-head-heart-spine, that is, remains authentic and stays connected to employees, change can be planned effectively. The leader will be close enough to the action to know when to fine-tune plan specifics, when to slow down or speed up, when to be direct and when to simply "walk the talk." Change is not synonymous with chaos, and having a plan for effective leadership is not the same as announcing a program with a new name or catchy slogan.

Grounded in strong sponsorship and a clear statement of vision, as Peter began his change effort in Chapter 1, managers and supervisors can begin the change process by having individual conversations with their direct reports, especially where employees work independently of each other.[34] Useful questions will include:

- What's working well?
- What's not working well?

+ Are there times when your work is delayed because you have to check with me?
+ Are there certain decisions you would like to make yourself?
+ Do you need additional training, information or resources to do this?
+ Are you willing to help me think through appropriate boundaries and checks and balances so that I can discharge my supervisory function effectively while giving you more autonomy in your work?

These questions can be used effectively with both salaried and hourly employees and with groups, where using a facilitator is often helpful. Group sessions can clarify and summarize previous informal chats. They can also explain after the fact changes that have been implemented without fanfare, like Howard's simply giving each employee the opportunity to order his/her own materials.

Before any of this can be effective, however, the work relationship between supervisor and employees needs to be an open one. For example, without handling serious rifts such as the one between Clem and his employees in Chapter 6, activities like those described here will be a charade.

In addition, when a manager begins asking these sorts of questions and listening to the responses, the pot is stirred and at some level change begins. Simple actions can intervene in the *status quo*. However, effective and lasting change needs a strategy and a healthy determination to stay the course.

An Action Plan

These conversations between supervisor and employees can be based on some solid data gathering by the manager/supervisor which might precede and serve to prompt the conversations:[35]

1. Using the Stages of Autonomy (Figure 4 in Chapter 4) profile, each leader (manager/supervisor) asks:

- ✦ Which profile best defines my unit?
- ✦ Which profile do I think most of my employees prefer?
- ✦ Which profile do I believe I am equipped to lead?

2. Rate your group/crew/direct reports using a ten to zero scale where ten represents a world-class score, the very best. A zero represents the opposite. The scores should be verifiable by hard data.
   - ✦ Rate each group on the following criteria:
   - ✦ Safety
   - ✦ Costs
   - ✦ Quality

A word about these three categories. Think of safety in expanded ways. Certainly physical safety is critical. How about emotional health? Is it safe to be an authentic self in this work environment? What degree of stress seems consistently present? What about burn-out? What about other indices of stress: How clear are the decision-making boundaries? Is sponsorship and support weak or strong? What degree of blaming occurs in the work environment? Is there any nutritional and preventive health encouragement in the work environment?

3. Add the three ratings together. If you have scored high, it may not be wise to move this group toward the next profile to the right. Suppose your group scores high on quality, safety, and costs and is a Profile 1? Can you imagine how disastrous it would be if you suddenly moved them to Profile 4 or, worse yet, a profile to the right of 4 where all supervision is removed? Our data suggest that your score will usually be higher as you move to the right, but it also shows that some traditional groups (Profile 1 or even 2) do perform very well and employees do feel respected. Apparently, they enjoy this more dependent style where they are told what to do

and simply go do it. However, such employees will probably shift gradually over time as they choose to pick up this or that decision-making opportunity.

4. Having scored the group responses, you are now ready to answer the next question. If it is advisable to move one profile number to the right, what would it take? What does this demand of me, the manager/supervisor? What do I need to do more of? What less of? How do I best monitor? What checks and balances should there be? When do I intervene? What training do I need? What does this demand of my employees? What should they do more of? Less of? What training do they need?

Each supervisor needs to do this homework for an estimate as well as for stimulation about possibilities. The real work on current decision styles and a desirable next stage will take place with the work group in one-on-one informal conversations and/or by meeting with the employees together: "How is it going today?" "How do you want it to be?" Out of the dialogue stimulated by these questions will emerge the leader's decision about the next step towards increasing autonomy and decreasing supervision. With such an evolution some supervisors will eventually have several groups—not just one.

5. At this stage, it's useful to analyze the decision-making action in your unit to (1) see more exactly what's going on on a regular basis and (2) prepare the way to make changes in the existing decision structure. The Decision Matrix[36] shown in Figure 6 will help identify where the "stuck points" are, that is, where do we drag our feet and fail to make decisions in a timely manner? (In the software industry, lack of decision-clarity about who makes "features" decisions is an issue that has cost tens of millions of dollars to some firms and ruined others.)

FIGURE 6: DECISION MATRIX—A SINGLE-POINT ACCOUNTABILITY WORKSHEET

Working Issues Requiring Decisions	Who Decides	Who is Consulted Prior to Decision?	Who Carries Out the Action	Who Needs to be Informed?	By When?
1.					
2.					
3.					
4.					
5.					

The "who decides" column never lists a group but always only one person chosen because of a combination of technical capability, strategic understanding of the consequences of the decision and enough personal internal authority to make a decision in the face of the inevitable resistance. If it's a "stuck point" that predictably will delay production, then there are differences about what decision should be made. Therefore, a decision is a "yes" to some persons and a "no" to others.

Another benefit of the decision matrix is that it may bring to light practices that are underground and sometimes destructive (the "Who Needs to be Informed" column can hold surprises). As a tool, then, the matrix can help a manager to see clearly how decision activity takes place in the unit at present and how it needs to be changed to promote productivity and to decrease schedule slippage.

6. Change, measure, adjust, measure—these are the next steps. Let performance measurements help you decide whether and how quickly you move to a new decision-making structure and when to intervene to correct cost/productivity, quality, or safety practices. The short story *Checks and Balances In Action* in Part Four underlines not only the value of data to a manager but an excellent way to use the data with an employee.

Moving in this way toward the right of the profile chart increases the chance of successful change but also increases the possibility of sustaining the change. However, since first-line supervisors are often chosen because they don't "make waves," many are also ill-equipped to take the steps suggested here.[37] What follows is a summary, written by Donald F. Simonic[38] of ALCOA, of what is required for effective delegation.

DELEGATION

In today's business environment, a strong leader must delegate in order to achieve maximum performance. Assigning decision-making authority, accountability, and freedom to act to others cannot be done in an arbitrary manner because one reads in a book that delegation is in vogue. Delivering power to subordinates must be prefaced by determining the maturity of the organization and its readiness for such steps and by identifying what the recipients need to be successful in their new roles.

There are at least four initiatives that must be completed before delegation can begin with some degree of certainty that it will add value:

1. Assessment

It is extremely important to evaluate those employees who are going to be assigned single-point accountability. The key is to select individuals who demonstrate at least the following characteristics in their day-to-day work lives:

Communication. They receive and provide information that is relevant, timely and that increases knowledge and understanding of the goals, competition, visions, values, direction of the business, and that builds ownership within the workforce.

Motivation. They provide a challenge to the organization to change through quantum leap goals.

Customer Focus. They understand customer requirements and meet them efficiently and effectively.

Initiative. They go beyond what their position requires.

Judgement. They possess good reasoning skills and act appropriately.

Self-Confidence. They state their own views, resolve conflict, deal with senior management effectively, and are always ready for a challenge.

Tenacity. They do whatever it takes, consistent with corporate values, to get the job done.

Some employees will be stronger in some areas and weaker in others. The important point is to look for people who exhibit the success factor and display evidence that they can be trained in those areas that need strengthening.

2. Training

Before providing leadership training, the manager or executive must first decide whether s/he wants an organization of supervisors (in the traditional sense) or of leaders. This is an extremely important issue because the latter is much more difficult to attain, but the rewards are greater. Supervising is much easier—telling people what to do, then watching over them to see that they do it. This, of course, does not build commitment or ownership in the employee ranks but will work to some degree as long as the supervisor micro-manages the work.

In contrast, leadership is much more difficult to pull off and is risky, since it requires delegation of power which reduces the manager's comfort zone. To lead well, it is necessary to state clear goals, engage in dialogue, stay the course against resistance, monitor (not micro-manage) the work, release resources, and be willing to reprimand and eager to validate.

Leadership skills cannot be injected with one dose of training. Developing world-class leaders takes time but can be accomplished with a well developed and executed training program. Training should include, but not be limited to, instruction and practice regarding single-point accountability, conflict resolution, decision-making, coaching, problem-solving, counseling, and checks and balances.

3. Boundary Specification

The third step in delegation is defining boundaries that specify freedom to act and make decisions. It is extremely important that limits be defined clearly and crisply to avoid misunderstanding regarding expectations. This should be done individually, employee-by-employee (or direct report-by-direct report) so that ultimately, upon agreement, single-point accountability will be established.

4. Checks and Balances

Last, but not least, as the manager disperses power and increases his/her span of leadership, measurements (checks and balances) must be defined and closely monitored to specifically evaluate performance against goals. I suggest objective measures that eliminate confusion and measure specific expectations and goals. Periodic, not less than quarterly, reviews should be undertaken that measure leadership skills in conjunction with performance accomplishments.

Delegation does not mean abdicating one's responsibility. Strong leadership goes hand-in-hand with high accountability and fosters high performance and high autonomy in successful organizations. It encourages pride of ownership, mutual support, openness, and authenticity.

It's an art *and* a science.
It's Leadership.

> A good story about delegation is ***Checks And Balances In Action***. Also see ***Appendix E: Delegation***.

CHAPTER 6

Conflict Resolution: When Boss and Employee Don't Dance

The individual manager can do much to shape his work unit climate, but sometimes the trust is so low and the communication so bad that the manager needs help from a third-party facilitator.[39]

In this chapter, you are invited to observe a skilled facilitator—Art Merlin of Peter's Story—assisting a manager and his work group of six supervisors. The incident relayed here, with names changed, actually happened, and it is such a common experience that several groups may think it was primarily written about them. The early dialogue in the narrative may be familiar to the reader. It reflects the usual hopelessness in such situations. The later responses are predictable only with skilled leadership.

Merlin had been working with Peter's company for three months when this intervention took place. The six floor supervisors in the plant reported to Clem Wilson, the manager of operations. Earlier, these six had completed a Survey Feedback Questionnaire. They, along with Clem, are about to meet with Merlin to analyze the data and problem-solve ways to work more effectively together.

The survey data indicated extremely low scores on many of the issues relating to the way they were supervised, the way they received communication about decisions, the sense of authority they had to do their jobs, and their overall job satisfaction.

Merlin began by talking first with Clem, then with each of his supervisors individually. Then, following an opening "sponsor" statement by Clem, Merlin met alone with the supervisors to discuss the situation. Trust was so low that Merlin had recommended dealing with manager-supervisor issues prior to taking up other issues raised by the survey data. Otherwise, the work would simply be superficial. And so Merlin begins "dance class":

"Hi, good to see you. I believe we have tough and, potentially, fruitful work ahead," Merlin says as he seats himself among the supervisors. He is greeted by silence and notices the supervisors' slumped body postures. "You don't seem ready to do this?"

"Are you kidding? This whole thing's a crock and a waste of time!" bellows Frank, a heavy-set supervisor. "Look, we don't have anything against you, personally."

Another supervisor, Mary, chimes in, "But forget it, our boss is hopeless."

Still another says, "Clem's been on our case for years. Do you expect us to believe that anything will be different just because we do this touchy-feely junk?"

"Well," responds Merlin, "I'd really be surprised if you did believe it would be different. It sounds like it's tough around here."

"You bet it's tough! How would you like someone snooping over your shoulder all the time, never trusting you? Would you like that?"

Merlin's gestures communicate that he understands the futility the supervisors feel.

"Hey man, we've done fun-and-games like this here before. But this is the real world, not the world you write about in your books. And this 'make it work' crap is just crap. We've been blamed a thousand times in the last year. Do you expect us to pretend that doing your funny little tricks is going to change him?"

Still another complains, "We've often talked to his boss; we used to turn in suggestion slips. But nothing's helped."

Another supervisor interrupts, "You know what might really change if we do this? I'll tell you what will change, our jobs will change. He'll can us. That's the only thing that's possible."

"Well, I certainly don't want to cause you any more trouble than you already live with day after day," Merlin says.

There is a pause, then Merlin rises and moves toward the door, saying, "I'll call Clem and tell him we won't be having the joint session with him."

"You'll what?" Mary asks.

"I'll tell him it isn't going to work to have any recommendations from you to him," Merlin repeats himself.

"What if he asks why?" Frank wonders.

"Well, I'll tell him the truth—that it seems hopeless and a waste of time."

"Geez, you can't tell him that!" they all agree.

"Well, then what shall I tell him?"

More silence.

"Well, if we decide to do this, what would we have to do?" Frank asks. "Are you really crazy enough (light laughter) to think you could do something?"

"I've got some crazy in me, yeah. Not that I can work magic. That's in your hands. If you so choose, I think I could help you do something to make it better."

"Like what?" They're still suspicious but the tone is changing.

"You've already done the first thing, and you've done really well. Do you realize how important it is to have had this conversation—a no-B.S. talk about how hopeless you feel about the situation?"

"Hell, we've been doing this every day for years." Now there is laughter as the tension eases.

"Can I say something honest?" asks Mary.

"Shoot."

"Sometimes, like when you just said 'you've done real well' you sound like a big phony to me. Like you're just here to do a job and make big consultant bucks. And sometimes you say things funny."

"Wow. I'm going to say something now that may also seem a little weird; it may even sound like a lie. But I really appreciate courage, and I think it took a lot of courage to say what you just said. And so I want to thank you. Thanks."

The supervisor looks surprised, and the tension in her face fades.

Merlin continues, "I'm sure nobody likes to be called a phony. And I certainly don't. But I can see how you might think I'm a phony at times. I'm sure I do speak a different way—sort of a communication jargon way that feels natural to me but sounds phony to you. Also, I *have* been a phony about at least one thing here today. I really want to succeed with you and your manager and I'm trying to act cool. But I'm nervous—this is really tough and I've been trying to hide that." Merlin pauses. "Well, Mary, did you ever have anyone thank you for calling him a phony?"

Mary laughs and says, "You really thanked me for being honest!"

"Exactly!"

Another pause, as Merlin gauges the climate in the room.

"Look, this whole conversation illustrates an incredible point about what your plant boss is encouraging: employee involvement. When one of you makes a suggestion to your supervisor–No, let me put it another way. When one of your own employees makes a suggestion to you, there are two things that need to be present for people-participation to work. First and foremost, you let them know that you appreciate their talking to you and telling you whatever it is they have to say. Use whatever is your best way—with a smile, by pausing and really looking at them, or by saying so—but you let them know you appreciate it.

"Then the second thing is, and these two things must be separated, you respond to whatever they say. For instance, the story is told about workers on an assembly line who can pull a certain cord to stop production if they think something is wrong. Now imagine that somebody pulls the cord, and the whole line is shut down. The first thing that happens is that the supervisor comes by and says to the worker: 'Thank you for calling attention to what you think is a problem.' Second, they look into the problem. Now it may or may not turn out to have been a problem, but can you imagine what would happen if the supervisor then chewed out that worker for pulling the cord?

"A major reason why there are unreported problems in organizations is that people are sometimes chewed out for mentioning them, especially if it turns out that the particular problem wasn't serious. When that happens—from then on—workers just don't report anything. So thank people for contributing. Then respond to the content and emotion of their statement. Well, that's a long explanation of something, right in the middle of everything we're working on here. But I think you can see how important it is."

A supervisor asks with an incredulous tone, "Are you claiming that Clem will say thank you?"

"No, not at all. No claims—but hopes, yes hopes. What I just said is a big picture of what I'm hoping will happen in your whole company eventually. But let's get back to Clem. It sounds like you don't want me to tell him there will be no report."

"What else can we do, Merlin?" says a supervisor.

"Well, there is something else. I need one of you, two of you, preferably everybody, but I need at least one or two of you to make a commitment. And you do it this way. You do it by just telling me, in your own words, that you make a personal commitment to improve the quality of the work relationship with Clem."

"How will that help?"

"I know that in situations like this, there is no possibility of change without personal commitment. It's like if your kid breaks her leg. You'll get her to the emergency room no matter what, because you have that commitment. Even if your car breaks down you'll get her there somehow, no matter what. I need someone here who says 'No matter what, I'm willing to make a commitment to improve the quality of the work relationship with Clem.'"

"Look, you don't get it. I hate this guy after what he's done to us. I'll never like him!" Frank is unmoved.

"The good news is that you don't have to like him—ever. You can hate him forever! What I'm asking is for a commitment to improve the quality of the *work* relationship!"

The room is silent as the supervisors glance at each other.

Frank slams his hand down on his knee and says, "Well, I'll do it! I can't stand it the way it is and the way it's been, and I'm willing to make that commitment."

"Great. Congratulations," Merlin says smiling.

Another supervisor says, "Me, too."

Merlin turns to look at this person. "OK. This may seem like a little game here, but are you willing to play the game with me and just state that commitment?"

"Sure, why not," he says. "I'm making a commitment to make things better with Clem."

"Thank you." Then, looking to another supervisor, Merlin asks, "And you?"

"Sure, just like what Frank said. Like, it's just gotta be better with Clem. I'll do everything I know how to do."

"Thank you. Who else? Is there anyone else who wants to make, maybe not wants to, but is willing to make that commitment?"

Mary goes next, two others follow suit, with the sixth hedging, "I'll wait and see how it works out."

With the commitments stated, Merlin invites the six to talk more about their work relationships with Clem. Of course, they had often gossiped with each other, so little was said that was new to anyone.

Merlin believed that such "venting" was a necessary first step before he could begin the task of helping them move from blaming to concreteness. But soon folks were giving illustrations in a non-blaming way, albeit with much help from Merlin. Getting them to own their part in this unhappy dance with Clem was more difficult. Merlin didn't want to appear to be siding with Clem, and yet he wanted these six to shift from a purely victim/blaming stance and begin to get a glimpse of how they—along with Clem—have co-created the situation.

Merlin chose not to take notes. He wanted each person to take responsibility for his/her own notes and, later, his/her own reporting. Above all, Merlin wanted Clem and the supervisors to develop the capacity to talk to each other and work out conflicts.

After a brief pause, Merlin says, "I think it's about time to go get Clem."

"What for?"

"I need to bring him here to talk about his and your commitments and these things we've been discussing."

"Now? Do you need to do it right now?" several supervisors chorus.

"Well, we could sit here silently for a while, take some deep breaths and *then* do it." They laugh. "OK, here I go, ready or not. Count to ten." Merlin leaves the room.

Anxiety is present in the room and skepticism remains high, but there is also a certain levity. Merlin's playfulness apparently inspires the group to have some fun about the situation.

Merlin walks down the hall to have Clem paged. Clem comes on the phone a moment later, and Merlin tells him that he would like very much to see Clem in Clem's office. Could he come in five minutes?

"You bet," responds Clem.

Clem takes a couple minutes to step into his boss's office and explain that he and his group are about to meet. Clem's boss has specifically requested that he cooperate with Merlin and is standing by, if needed, to support the work. This situation has long been rumored throughout the plant, so there are hardly any secrets about the enmity between Clem and his supervisors. Clem's boss was no longer willing to make Clem's participation in correcting the situation voluntary.

In Clem's office, Merlin speaks first:

"Clem, I have good news for you. Your people have just made a commitment to improve the quality of their work relationship with you."

Clem's eyes open wide. Merlin continues:

"I'm imagining that you, too, would want to make that same commitment to them."

Clem responds with a sense of relief, "You bet!"

"Clem, it looks like it's been really rough."

"Yeah! I never believed when I took this job that it would be this hard."

"OK, " Merlin suggests, "let's go down to the room and meet the group. When we get there, I'm going to ask you to share your commitment with them to improve the quality of the work relationship. OK?"

"OK."

The anxiety is high as Merlin and Clem enter the room where the six supervisors are seated in a rough circle of chairs. Polite "hellos" are exchanged. Clem and Merlin each take an empty chair, and Merlin dives right in.

"OK. We're here to make your work relationship better. Everybody admits it's been lousy, and I've asked you, Frank, to say to Clem what we agreed on."

Frank proceeds: "Clem, it's been really lousy between you and us, and I, for one, am making a commitment to improve things. I don't want to live this way any longer at work. It's affecting me at home, everywhere. So that's my commitment to you."

Two or three other supervisors follow suit with similar statements, and the others nod their heads. Their attention is riveted on Clem. The catch in Clem's throat is apparent.

"I don't like the way it's been either, and I blame myself a lot for it. I guess I don't know how to manage. It's been no good, and I'm telling you I'm sorry, and I'm going to do everything I know how to do to make it better. I'll do my best."

At this point, Merlin is encouraged about what will happen next. His experience in similar situations has led him to believe that when this kind of beginning is made—no matter how bad the conflict has been or how long it has lasted—the chances of success are greatly enhanced.

Commitment is fundamental to success at all levels, whether it is a mid-level manager with supervisors or the chief executive with the vice-presidents. That commitment has to be made intentionally, has to be clearly spoken, and be clearly understood. Whether it is a commitment to improve work relationships, to improve product quality, or to exceed customer expectations, it needs to be clearly stated.

Also, it is important that the participants verbalize their commitment in their own language. If the supervisors and Clem had refused to state their determination to improve their work relationship, the consultant would not have moved forward with his plan. No matter how good the process, it is the intent of the participants that is critical to the eventual outcome. Each must understand that s/he is a co-creator of the situation. Waiting for the other to change doesn't work. Each must take his/her own responsibility and individual steps.

Successfully dealing with conflict is not a matter of hope, not a matter of having a logical step-by-step approach, and not a matter of having a clever consultant. Rather, it is fundamentally a matter of clear intentionality and commitment by those involved in the problem.

Commitment means we've only just begun, and yet, what a beginning! That initial declaration is like pushing a sled from the top of the hill and getting the momentum started. You may have only gone a few feet, but your likelihood of getting to the bottom of the hill is exceedingly high.

After Clem and the supervisors voiced their commitment, Merlin indicates that the group needs to get into specifics. What exactly are we talking about? Again, there is an awkward silence until Frank pounds his fist and said "O.K. I'll tell you."

And he begins a story of how Clem is always interrupting, about how he would be in his office talking to another person when Clem would walk in and sit down and sit there without speaking until the other person left. Mary tells about how Clem lingers outside her door and listens to her telephone conversations and is, she says, trying to spy on her. All the supervisors describe how they, too, think Clem spies on them. They talk about the numerous times Clem walks down the hall past the supervisors' offices, which are free-standing partitions with panels on the bottom and glass on top. They believe that this demonstrates how he lacks trust in them, and holding on to that belief as the "truth about Clem," they deeply resent him.

Clem is obviously stunned.

Merlin asks, "Clem, when you walk down the hall past the row of supervisors' offices, and you see one of them talking to somebody else, what goes through your head?"

Clem responds, eager to clarify: "Well, these people are tough to get hold of, even with our walkie-talkies, and when I want to discuss something in depth, I know that if I don't stay right outside their door or sit down in the chair there, that in a few minutes they'll dash out of their office to somewhere in the plant, and I'll have missed them. So I just very quietly sit down and wait."

There is astonished disbelief in the room, but then gradually people begin to see that, from Clem's perspective, he wasn't spying—he needed to communicate with them, to catch them before they flew away—but still their skepticism continues.

One participant says, "I have trouble believing that you aren't spying."

Merlin says, "That's O.K. You don't have to believe he wasn't spying. Clem, they don't have to believe you weren't spying. I have good news for everyone—there is a very simple solution to this problem: All we have to do now is find out how Clem can get messages to you without sitting on the chair or without overhearing your telephone calls. We don't have to go back and rework the past. We just have to make sure, in the future, that Clem's messages get delivered in a way that works for each of you."

At this point in the process, it is very important not to bring up or try to sort out past incidents. Future success is about what will happen from now on, not what happened in the past—and certainly not about "proving" or "disproving" interpretations of past events. Whether he was "spying" or "being conscientious" lies in the realm of opinion, not fact.

So they worked out a procedure for Clem to get messages to his supervisors when he walked through their office corridor and saw through the glass partition that the supervisors were with someone or on the phone. Clem suggested that he give a signal—he would touch his right ear, meaning he had a message. The supervisor could either wave him in to sit down or raise an open palm which meant wait outside just a minute. They had great fun inventing this code, even adding a few irreverent suggestions that gave everyone a chuckle, including Clem.

The supervisors then agreed on specific follow-throughs for the next three Fridays when they would meet and talk about the questions on their regular agenda: Has this happened? What's going on? What's working well? What isn't working? It seemed that everyone felt good about the outcome.

Just before the meeting ends, Merlin mentions that he has been timing a ten-minute period during the meeting beginning when the first supervisor had accused Clem of spying. Merlin steps up to the blackboard on the wall, grabs a piece of chalk, and draws a large version of the letter "L" with the base of the "L" extended longer than is typical. He labels the vertical axis with the word "Tension" and labels the horizontal axis "Time" and ticks off increments of 2, 4, 6, 8, and 10 minutes along the horizontal axis. (See Figure 7.)

Then he says, "Now, when Frank first accused Clem, how many felt tension?" Everyone raises a hand.

"How high was your tension?"

The group indicates that it was extremely high. Merlin draws a small "X" at the zero-minutes mark high on the tension scale. "O.K. Now, at about the fourth minute Clem told his part of the story, that he hadn't had spying in his mind but rather wanted to deliver a message. How much tension did you feel then?"

FIGURE 7: MERLIN'S DIAGRAM

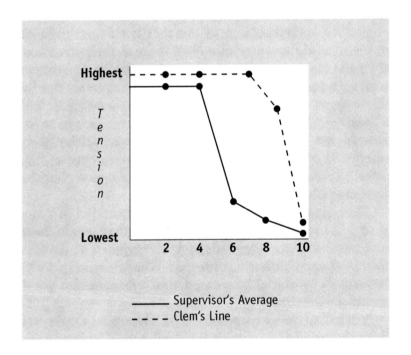

"Oh, tension dropped a lot," the supervisors agree.

Merlin draws a small "X" above the four-minute mark medium way up the tension scale. "Now, how about the tenth minute when I announced the good news—that all we needed now was to find a solution in the future. How was the tension then?"

The supervisors report that their tension was nearly zero. Merlin draws a small "X" low on the tension scale above the ten-minute mark and then draws a sharply declining line connecting the "Xs".

Then he asks Clem about his tension line. Clem says that it was very high when Frank accused him and remained high while Clem spoke but then started to decline more gradually. Clem's line didn't drop as fast as the group's, but, also, by the tenth minute, his tension was greatly reduced.

"Compared to the tension you felt when Frank slammed his fist and accused Clem, what's been the tension level the last few months?" Merlin asks.

People chortle and one corrects Merlin with "You mean the last few years! Well, it's been right up there at the top of the blackboard. We've been living with this tension for over two years."

Two years! This group attempted to work for two years with high tension. Because they were focusing on Clem as a "personality problem," they believed the situation was hopeless; yet in ten minutes from the time Frank banged his fist until they began searching for the solution to how messages could be delivered, the tension dropped dramatically.

It's not always that easy to pinpoint and solve the conflict, especially when, based on the statements of many people in the plant, this "spy" accusation was both believed to be a "fact" and was the most notorious dysfunctional relationship story in the company.

For several weeks following this initial session, the group of six met weekly with Merlin and Clem. They reported that the finger signals were working, they were having many individual conversations with Clem, and things indeed were much better. No additional changes needed to be made, they all agreed that communications were good, and the consultant did not need to meet with the group any longer. With the increased trust which resulted from this work, they were not only solving productivity and quality problems with reasonable ease, but were also leading (in the crews reporting to the six supervisors) in important indices such as safety, cost reduction, and production efficiency.

A year later, Merlin happened to see Frank in the plant cafeteria and inquired how things were. By then, one of the supervisors had become a fishing companion of Clem's. The effect on the whole department, including employees supervised by the six supervisors, was still positive. A source of raw tension was gone.

In addition to the *commitment* each person made, two other factors made this intervention successful: a skilled *facilitator* and a clear *conflict-utilization process.*

The role of the outside consultant was obviously crucial, but that role might also have been played by an internal consultant, manager, or employee.[40] However, to be effective, such a person needs to be trained in some of the third-party conflict skills used by most outside consultants. To be an effective third party and help resolve issues, the consultant—internal or external—needs to do certain things well:

KEY ELEMENTS OF EFFECTIVE CONFLICT UTILIZATION

1. Bring oneself to the work.

The third-party consultant needs to show up as a self striving for authenticity, not as a technique-pusher. While there are important process steps, trust develops from the ability of the third-party—in the midst of an anxious, conflicted system—to be authentic.

2. Listen without defending.

During Merlin's work with Clem and his group, the process and the consultant came under attack time after time during the early sparring period. The consultant understood that it was not his function to make the group members believe anything. The consultant also understood that, if they were cynical about the process or the goals, it was not his function to either argue about or ignore their cynicism or their attacks.

3. Maintain perspective.

Throughout, it is important to keep clearly in perspective the macro goals of employee involvement in the whole organization. At one stage, Merlin risked making a point about the courage to say "thank you" and the need to appreciate people's contributions separate from one's judgment about the quality and substance of what they say. Doing so placed this situation within the larger context of the organization's change strategy of involving all employees more significantly in the use of their expertise. If such conflict work is done in an organization without a larger framework, it will be like simply putting out fires. It will seem isolated from the real work of production. And it will lack support from upper management who will be embarrassed that such a situation exists rather than excited and pleased about the humane and productive consequences of this conflict work.

Just as with individually-focused training, such conflict work is like a "voice crying in the wilderness" when there is no clear direction, no mission, no dynamic organization, no broad movement towards improved safety/productivity/quality/morale and no acknowledgment that such conflicts are natural in organizations, families, and life. When this larger framework exists, Clem and his group will be proud of their achievement. When they are not present, the group will be ashamed that it was singled out. Indeed, the chances of the group doing such conflict work—let alone doing it effectively—will be greatly reduced. Who will make a commitment to improvement in a company without the company itself making the same commitments guided by the vision, behavior, and, yes, commitment of the CEO?

4. Keep the consultant role clear.

The consultant knew—because the company had initiated this process—that the employees were between the proverbial rock and a hard place. They could either work the issue or refuse to work the issue, but they could not refuse to work the issue and just drift into the woodwork. If they refused to work the issue, such refusal had to be confronted and communicated to management—they had to tell somebody besides the consultant. So, one way or the other, an aspect of the issue had to be handled. The supervisors began to see this reality when they stopped the consultant from telling the boss there would be no report.

The consultant is an agent, not the sponsor, of the change and, knowing this clearly, he did not get into a persuasive mode. It was not his problem! Yet he also did not make avoidance easy.

5. Refuse to buy into "interpretation" by parties to the conflict.

The supervisors said, "...Our boss is hopeless." The consultant later reflected, "...It seems hopeless." They said Clem "spied" and didn't trust them. The consultant gestured to acknowledge their sense of futility. He recognized their interpretations as their unique way of telling their story. Later he guided them away from their unique interpretation (held by them not only as the "truth" but as a definitive view of Clem) to the identification of specific behaviors.[41]

6. Reflect the emotional level.

Though it's difficult to detect emotions in a written story such as this, it is important to note that the facilitator responded in a "hot" tone and posture to "hot" statements. A clinically-appearing facilitator may be less credible to those workers who easily express emotion. More reserved facilitators can develop the more expressive side of themselves and expressive facilitators can learn to be more reserved.

7. Constantly move toward a future focus.

The past may need to be touched lightly, but it will not be unraveled. Efforts to prove one party was wrong are utterly fruitless and, most often, escalate the conflict. No one has to think or believe anything different about what has been, but the future is not determined by the past. It is influenced by decisions and commitments made now. Critical to success are the development of specific future behaviors, agreements, and follow-through plans.

8. Follow steps in effective conflict-utilization.[42]

Here are the general conflict-resolving steps which Merlin followed:

- Clarify that this work is sponsored by, in this case, Clem and his boss. Without clear sponsorship, the work has little chance of success. Otherwise, Merlin will tend to make it his problem and over-function (persuade, threaten, coerce, manipulate, over-trust technique);
- Become aware of the specific problems through individual conversations;
- Encourage private commitment to improve the *work* relationship;
- Share those commitments;
- Ventilate the issue(s);
- Get the parties talking directly to each other, not primarily through the consultant;
- Clarify the issue(s) and help each other see it from the other's perspective. Make clear that the story is his or hers, each is unique so there's no point in arguing about the other person's story;

- Search for reciprocal agreements, that is, both parties to the conflict have a part in the resolution, not just the conflict;
- State solution decisions in clear, behavioral, descriptive terms, with by-whens;
- Set dates for follow-through; and
- Follow up to see what happened and fix it if it doesn't work.

All of the above conditions were essential to moving Clem and his group from gossiping to problem-solving. The gossiping had been going on for two years. The solutions were conceived in a two-hour session from which everyone—Clem, the supervisors, and the whole company—emerged as winners.

CHAPTER 7

Structural Change: The Easy Way Out

"**Y**ou need to be sure you have the right people, the right number of people, and the most streamlined organizational structure possible." Merlin's statement replays itself in Peter's head, especially "the right number" part, as he walks into the Castle Cafe to meet his trusted advisor.

Peter's company is midway into the change process he designed, and he is disillusioned by how difficult it is to increase employee autonomy and responsibility. "Clearly we have too many salaried staff and too little clarity about expectations, let alone measurements" he mused, as he and Merlin sipped their lattes, "and with an average supervisor-to-employee ratio of one to seven, we are micro-managing!"

"And the solution would be?" Merlin asked, tilting his chair back as he scanned the Seattle waterfront.

"Downsizing, followed by a reorganization with better supervisor-employee ratios," Peter replied. "If they're delegating well, supervisors should be able to support several work groups/crews."

This is not an unusual direction for organizations to take. In fact, many companies think the best way to solve corporate problems is by changing the organization's structure. This new trend is quite reminiscent of my personal experience in the 1960s. At that time I was an employee in an organization that changed its structure three times in eight years. In the last three decades, my work as a consultant often meant picking up the pieces and dashed hopes of organizations where the "new" structure was sold as the answer to big problems. Often nothing changed:

- People were more confused about roles, responsibilities, and communication patterns.
- Productivity increased in only one out of four organizations.[43]
- Certain previous problems were reduced and new problems emerged.
- The foundation was laid for the next structural change a couple years down the road.

I have also seen new structures that enabled more effective work processes and eased certain problems. Certainly the shift from hierarchical, layered structures to those that support a leaner, more flexible organization is important in this fast-paced competitive world. But even when this is so, many organizations fail to implement well and suffer a longer productivity dip than necessary. They do not take into account the ensuing confusion resulting from the change or plan sufficient dialogue with those affected by the change. It is not unusual for employees to remain confused about reporting relationships, roles, and priorities for months, even years.

The purpose of organizational change is to arrange the structure so that processes are efficiently aimed towards maximal effectiveness. Organizational structural change aimed solely at cost reduction, empowerment of employees, duplication of changes elsewhere, or any other single or programmatic emphasis is doomed to fail. Also there are systemic issues that simply will not be solved by rearranging the boxes on an organization chart. While Peter might wish to hurry the change, the step he has embarked upon is probably the wisest course since it deals with key systemic issues, encourages less micromanagement, will sustain the change, and will still accomplish results much quicker than most can imagine.

Organizations are a series of interlocking triangles. First, I want to illustrate this interpersonally, then systemically. Interpersonally, Joe may be upset at John, but he tells Mary, as illustrated in Figure 8.

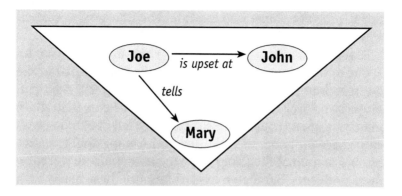

FIGURE 8: INTERPERSONAL TRIANGULATION

While letting off steam and searching for one's own clarity may be quite helpful for Joe prior to talking to John, the triangulation is dysfunctional when Mary and Joe consistently talk *about* John rather than *to* John. Breaking such dysfunctional patterns is critical for effective work unit functioning. Figure 9 illustrates such dysfunction in the larger system.

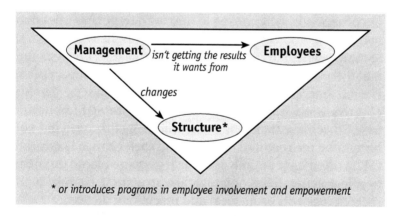

* or introduces programs in employee involvement and empowerment

FIGURE 9: SYSTEMIC TRIANGULATION

Management must focus on results, not activities. Often efforts to improve quality are measured, not by outcomes, but by how many attend a training. Likewise, downsizing is an activity, not an outcome. Organizations should be structured to support critical processes in the system that affect bottom-line results.

I believe that frequent structural change in an organization is due to the failure of management to be both empathic and decisive. Many managers do not deal openly with their employees and seek to manage as illustrated in Figure 9. In short, managers often create a new structure instead of working with employees on issues of authority, decision making, role clarity, and accountability. They hope the new structure will solve these problems, but then it doesn't because these issues are a product of unclear leadership, not structural deficiency.

Structural change, like training, is an activity. Effective organizations measure success by results, not activities or the arrangement of boxes on a chart. But while major structural change may be undertaken to avoid issues of effective management, it may also be a wise step. Streamlining by flattening the structure or restructuring only those parts that are dysfunctional can produce positive results.

In one company, a manager had an unusually high number of supervisors reporting to him with responsibilities that had little relationship to the scope of work he was expected to manage. He had collected a potpourri of direct reports and had little time or inclination to manage certain supervisors. His job description and reward system were not related to his effectiveness with these reports. Change seemed important here. To achieve that change the whole organization did not have to be restructured. Pinpointing such change is critical. CEO's often have entirely too much pressure placed on them to effect generalized organization structural change, as if such change will be magical and precipitate success.

Unresolved core management issues will continue to haunt such organizations through change after change. Structural change does not replace or eliminate the need for managers to manage and supervisors to supervise. In short, a boss is responsible and accountable. That is, a boss ensures clarity and uses authority appropriately to support an orderly and dynamic work environment. The boss learns by listening. An appropriate use of authority includes delegation and the creating of an open, non-blaming, problem-solving workplace.

Peter knew that what is critical to success is clarity about authority, decision-making (who decides, who is consulted), employee influence, single-point accountability (one person accountable, not two), tangible and intangible rewards, specific (what you did and said) feedback, and clarity about wants/expectations. The inability to do these things and deal with day-to-day conflict will result in inefficient utilization of resources. This pattern of inefficiency will continue to plague the organization no matter what the structure.

And speaking from an authentic "I" position is also critical. For example:

- ◆ "I need this to succeed on my job." ("What do you need?")
- ◆ "I expect this from you." ("What do you expect?")
- ◆ "I need this signed and in my hands by Tuesday noon in order to meet my deadline with my customers."

CROSS-FUNCTIONING, MATRIXED TASK FORCES

Much structural change is driven by the increasing cross-functional, matrixed, interdependent work groups of the 1990's. In organizations today, the kind of clarity discussed above is even more essential than in the old days of isolated departments and crews with simpler lines of authority.

Through a recent organizational change an executive attempted to resolve marketing and engineering issues in product development by combining two groups and declaring co-management by two individuals from different disciplines. In effect, a situation is created where either can veto the other. The history of such co-leadership or consensual decision-making is not a pretty one. The primary beneficiary is the most stubborn member. Whoever holds out the longest wins. Such "co-leadership" can only succeed if each leader has clear areas of decision authority and no decisions are jointly made. Consultation—yes—but decision authority must be single-point.

Cross-functional work where no one person is given single-point accountability will be disastrous no matter what the structure. Managerial and supervisory alignment about the task, priorities, resource allocation, and decision authority remains the critical component in any organizational structure. Much structural change is devised to make up for these types of insufficiencies in the existing structure, but these insufficiencies cannot be rectified by structural change because they are not issues of organization structure. Rather, they are both systemic and personal.

Perhaps an illustration about an inappropriate use of training will highlight my point about the possible misuse of structure change. Training programs are triangulated again and again. A manager might think, "I can't manage this person, so I will send him to that training and hope he will change." A consultant[44] was surprised when the client informed him that he would be leading several employees in a training session. One of the targeted employees reported to the client and had been a source of great difficulty and the consultant believed he had been hired to work with the client and that employee. The dialogue occurred as follows:

- **Consultant:** "Since you've announced the training I'll go ahead with it, but our firm won't bill you."
- **Client:** (Surprised) "Why not?"
- **Consultant:** "Because it won't help."
- **Client:** "What would help?"
- **Consultant:** "Cancel the training and I'll work with you and this employee and help you say to him what you've avoided saying."

The client canceled the training and accepted the consultant's offer. The temporary role of the consultant was to coach the manager in being specific with this employee about concerns, wants, and potential consequences—in short, to be authentic!

Training can assist but not if it is used as a substitute for managing. Emphases such as employee involvement or empowerment must be integrated into daily management practices. They are not just for hourly employees; they apply to everyone and represent good management practice. Programs about these emphases are often substituted for ineffective management that has failed to appropriately involve those with knowledge and experience in an influential way. Rather, managers, while intending well, have shifted to permissive, decision-making ambiguity rather than clearly managing the distinction between employee influence and decision-making.

The creation of certain rules for employees is another example of systemic triangulation in the workplace. How many rules have been imposed on *all* employees to handle violations by the *few* whose bosses have not managed with appropriate clarity and consequences?[45]

Only managers who both lead and stay connected with their people will manage a new structure well. Without one's own internal authority, a manager becomes a victim of dysfunctional systems issues rather than a creator and sustainer of a healthy system. The capacity to be such a strong leader and stay in touch with others in an empathic way is an art— a spiritual achievement of great practicality to the leader who wants to move towards his/her vision unstopped by resistance and sabotage.

To achieve success in structural change, management needs to:

- ♦ Focus on integrated goals that the change is expected to achieve— no single emphases.
- ♦ Imagine new configurations "outside the box." (In this world of computers and telephones, office location is less important.)
- ♦ Review structural ideas with impartial observers who will be less prone to depend on tradition or think in terms of personalities.

- Build your new structure with strong performers in key positions. Remember, the structure will not shore up weak managers.
- Carefully plan and execute the transition. Include facilitated sessions with new intact and cross-functional groupings in the plan as well as maximal dialogue between management and employees.
- Ensure that clarity about decision-making, priorities, accountabilities, and sponsorship are in place and reinforced as the structure shifts.
- Allow for differences among departments. Remember, it's not primarily the structure but how people believe in and manage the structure that is key. (True, some structures, such as those without single-point accountability, are almost impossible to manage.)
- Clarify those few things that must not be changed (for legal or other reasons); then put everything else up for grabs.
- Temper the "up-for-grabs" by constantly focusing on goals. Don't change for the sake of change.

Structural change can be effective and much more than simply "the easy way out" if managers will also do whatever difficult work is required—that is, lead. The next time someone suggests a major structural change as a solution, however, ask yourself, "Is making and remaking the structure a pattern in this company?" If the answer is "Yes," look elsewhere for a path. Look to clarity about authority and decision-making. Look to help managers become skilled in their own personal authority—speaking for themselves, saying "I" need/want/expect/think/ feel. Help them develop their capacity to listen deeply to others without being caught up by the perils of permissive management and pretend consensus.

By itself, structural change is the easy way out. No amount of box shuffling can substitute for effective leadership.

◆◆◆

Part Three
A Theory of Leadership

◆◆◆

CHAPTER 8

Leadership and Authenticity

This book was written for people who care about both *authenticity* and *productivity*. Those who would neglect either of these dimensions will find this book useless.

In the organization which values *authenticity* alone, people are encouraged to be "true to their inner selves" apart from any concern for work productivity. This kind of organization can become extremely cultish. It will be a place where honesty and complete self-disclosure become a true-belief tyranny that splits a company between the noble who "get it" and the ignoble who reject the "true way." Also, productivity will likely suffer.

The organization in which *productivity* is the single operative value, where there is little regard for authenticity and integrity, will be a soulless place fit only for those who either manage robots or who would treat humans as mere tools of the marketplace.

This book, then, is about the journey organizations can make to live fully in both dimensions and what *leadership* in such organizations looks like. Peter's Story illustrates the ways a designated leader can create a culture where people can be both authentic and productive by themselves embracing their own leadership in their day-by-day work life.

First, a disclaimer. Authenticity is neither a state that can be perfectly attained nor a state which—when attained— will always be a positive force. Actually, *attain* is a strange word here since all of us were born authentic. As babies, our internal states were instantaneously made manifest by our behavior. A smile may have reflected a happy state or a gas bubble, but it certainly did not mask anger. And when we were unhappy, we simply cried, and those around us didn't have to guess how we were feeling.

On a recent plane trip, I made the acquaintance of a six-month old infant. She sat quietly in her mother's lap and stared at me for an unusual length of time. I stared back. Her gaze was direct, straightforward, unblinking, and I envied her capacity to be present in the moment with apparently no pretense, no fear of the future, and no regrets.

However, it is clear what's in store for her. She will grow up. That is, she will be socialized. That marvelous, spontaneous capacity of hers must be tempered if she is to function among other humans. The unbridled authenticity of babyhood comes without clarity about boundaries with others. Putting one's inner thoughts and feelings directly on "external speaker" doesn't always work well in our day-to-day interactions with friends, co-workers, or even family.

Neither does the opposite extreme. The totally socialized human is so other-oriented that there is no self. Such a person has lost touch with those inner thoughts and feelings fairly completely in order to fit it. Most of us, however, simply edge ourselves part way along the balance beam, experiencing our true feelings when it suits our purposes, expressing them only occasionally. It is inevitable that the uncanny capacity of the baby to both be aware of feelings and instantaneously express them will be seriously compromised in the process of socialization.

The socialization of girls is different from that of boys. This is because the rules of adult life are different for men and women. For example, girls are encouraged to stay tuned, as they mature, to their nurturing capacity, that special listening for the needs of others. Boys are largely encouraged to disregard this more gentle aspect of their nature. Instead, their socialization occurs around conflict issues where they must choose to fight or to flee. What we often find, then, in the work place are women who value consensus over authentic disagreement and men who would rather be right (win) than be authentic (and truthful) "losers."

Women are sometimes not prepared for conflict and thus evidence avoidance behaviors like blaming or crying or attempting to appease others. Or they engage in outright denial—"I'm fine. There's nothing wrong." At the same time, men, in the face of family conflict, will often flee behind the newspaper or to the chair in front of the TV. (Where do you suppose the phrase "strong and silent type" came from?) And at the office they will fight by taking a defended stance which may be manifest in argumentative, stone faced, controlling behavior.

All of these behaviors—blaming, defending, "flighting", stonewalling—are masks of pretentiousness, the essence of *inauthenticity*. We carry these masks with us wherever we go, including work.

I believe that one can "become as a little child" and paradoxically still be an adult and make choices. Instead of putting on a mask or responding to another's defensiveness, one can simply say what's so, speaking without blame: "I'm troubled by the dip in production. Let's talk!"

Fundamentally, authenticity is simple. It is stating *your* truth (not *the* truth) without blaming. It cuts through the masks.

In looking for adults who not only will but can be authentic, the trauma and shaping of these early years must be addressed and transcended. By our late teens, we have often unknowingly allowed the false, pretentious self to take charge and so, of course, it shows up in the workplace.

Herein lies the problem. To be authentic, one must have the capacity of the very young child to be aware of one's emotions and thoughts and the capacity of the adult to make choices about appropriate behavior. The authentic self sends congruent messages. That is, one's words, tone, face, and gestures all match. Now here comes another paradox. The authentic *wise* self sometimes chooses inauthentic behavior. The predicted risks of total authenticity may, on occasion, seem too high, and one may choose, instead, to risk faking it. Both are risks.

But it is a choice—that is, for those who are self-aware. The unaware are confined to the hell of reactivity. You say this, I do that. You do that, I feel this. You *made* me do what I did or you *made* me feel what I felt. You blame. I blame back or I defend or flee or placate. It's your fault what I do or feel. I am not a self; I am a victim.

In the early 1960s, I was involved in training adults to work with youth, providing a particular emphasis on authenticity.[46] We emphasized the need for adults to learn to *be* rather than to *pretend* with young people. In order to do this, the adults needed to embrace a core quality called "striving for authenticity."

The "striving" part is important because authenticity is not a mountaintop we someday reach. It is a journey. For adults, it's about coming clean with youth. It exposes the phoniness in the older ones when they pretend to know more than they know, be who they are not, or deny the errors and inadequacies that are part of being human, whether younger or older.

Being authentic is knowing what you care about and standing up for that. It is being in touch with and owning your emotional states: fear, hope, joy, anger, love, hate, whatever. It is being aware of your defensiveness and acknowledging it and then choosing to defend or not defend rather than always reactively explaining yourself whenever you think you've been put on the spot.

Ruth Emory has written:

> The authentic individual will not pretend to stand on ground which is not in reality his/her ground.... This is really you, and not a "put-on" person. Authentic life means that people can feel able to trust you because they know you mean what you say and really are as you seem. There is an assurance that even though they may hate what you are and stand for, they can depend on it. You are no will-o'-the-wisp.

She adds that this core quality may be expressed in many ways:

> ♦ "Individuals are fully aware of their possibilities as well as their limitations," and do not deny them.

* "They are able to say that they do not know something and not be frightened by the necessity for such acknowledgment."

* Authentic individuals invite a critical scrutiny of their ideas and really welcome what comes without either supinely acquiescing or loudly defending.

* "They expect others to be authentic and they help them discover who they are and where they live, and are sensitive to—but not 'thrown' by—their inconsistencies as they find their personhood."

* They are open and able to receive messages about themselves without becoming unduly hostile or resentful.

* "They speak to others in the group honestly, from a wholeness of spirit."

* "They say what they truly believe to be the case insofar as they can see it, and not what they think they are expected to say; but they also speak responsibly, not out of whim or smallness of spirit."[47]

The authenticity Emory talks about begins with self-differentiation. Before I can be authentic, I must know who I am; I must distinguish between me and my family, my history, my judgments, my projections, and the external world. I must recognize that I construct my personal perception of "reality," or what's out there and admit that I don't know you by your actions but rather by my unique interpretation of you. Only then will I speak for myself and not believe that what I am experiencing is what everyone is or should be experiencing. My reality is not your reality. With such clarity I may avoid believing that my feelings are "our" feelings, my thoughts "our" thoughts, my perceptions "our" perceptions, my reality "our" reality! Authentic behavior is grounded in such differentiation.[48]

Authentic leaders speak the truth. They say "I" if it's "I" and "we" if it's "we." If they're talking about a group product, they refer to the authors as "we." If they're stating their own point of view, they say "I." They're truthful about their own authority and neither deny nor flaunt it. If they're asked "Are you the boss of this unit?" they say "Yes." They don't say "There's no boss— we're a team," if they really are the boss. They understand that legitimate leaders are needed. They know that leaders are no better or worse than other people. They simply are. And they know that leaders perform important functions—as parents, judges, presidents, police officers, teachers, bosses, union officers, shop stewards, pilots, and captains.

Striving for authenticity reduces the pretending, the game-playing way of being in the world. It opens the door for intimacy in relationships, for integrity in the marketplace, and for openness among people of differing backgrounds and with different roles.

The world today hungers for authentic leaders at all levels of our organizations. As used on these pages, the word *leader* means

> *A person with integrity and a high order of self-awareness who will decisively take risks and openly guide others into the unknown future.*

Note that this definition makes no reference to an individual's position or level in the organizational hierarchy, church, or family, implying that a leader may be found anywhere within the boundaries of a structure.

Thus, the title of this chapter might seem to tell it all. Almost. One can perhaps be authentic and not lead. However, *one cannot lead and not be authentic.* The inauthentic human can con others, steal from others, or force others, but not lead. In these pages, I reserve the right to demand authenticity of those who would lead. And more.

The core of this approach is the development of the capability to "be a self and stay connected" with others. Human development, at least through the teen years, is characterized by the child's tendency to solve dilemmas in the parent-teacher-child authority relationship by dependency ("I'll do what I'm told") or counter-dependency ("Don't tell me what to do" or "Tell me this and I'll do something else") or cut-off

("I'll run away from home" and later "I'll move a thousand miles away from home"). The imbalance between being a self (which sometimes means that one must take an unpopular stand, that is, say "no" when the other wants a "yes") and staying connected in an empathic, caring way is carried into adult life and certainly manifested at work, especially in the boss-employee relationship.

Authenticity, as discussed here, represents the striving to achieve a cyclical balance between the self as unique and the fundamental connection not only with parents, bosses, and all other humans but with the cosmos. In one way, I am unique like the story of the just born Buddha who immediately took seven steps and said, "There's no one in the world like me." Perhaps all babies are baby Buddhas and their first cry signals their uniqueness. Ironically, the journey of adulthood is the rediscovery of that elemental truth.

Likewise, we are all connected. Perhaps this is our primary essence. You and I are one. All life is a manifestation of the same energy. Thus, striving for authenticity is not a solitary pursuit but rather a pursuit in relationship. Otherwise, one is trapped in a lonely valley hearing only the sound of one's echo. Authenticity is not to be confused with "rugged individualism." In one's most authentic moments, one can take a stand without disconnecting from others and can give oneself to a significant cause, a meaningful vision, and a larger community without losing self. Robert Greenleaf has written, "...The great leader is seen as a servant first, and that simple fact is the key to greatness."[49] Being a self/taking a stand and staying connected are cyclical: like "the chicken and the egg" neither precedes or follows the other. They are interrelated.

Ultimately, you and I will discover that the connection is not only with humans but in and with the web of life, with the cosmos. We are evolving—not on the planet but with the planet. We are interconnected. We are one or we are no one. Thus, the authentic leader measures integrity not only in people relationships but in environmental care and a sense of cosmic purpose. After speaking about the care of the self, Joseph Campbell astutely remarks that this is "... only the second law of life. The first law is that you and the other are one."[50]

And while money and material riches can be manipulated by the inauthentic, in the long run people are motivated to work for and be loyal to those whom they trust: authentic leaders.

Can such authentic leadership be trained or, rather, re-awakened with an adult perspective and capacity to choose appropriate authenticity? Yes! In fact, this book is about the development of leaders who are authentic, that is, people who are (reasonably) in touch with their

+ Guts—emotion, intuition;
+ Head—thinking, making meaning, clarifying;
+ Heart—passion, vitality, caring; and
+ Spine—courage, decisiveness, taking a stand; so that they become *choice-makers*, *creators*, and *visionaries* who therefore
+ Set clear goals that stretch themselves and others;
+ Stay the course against resistance;
+ Create alignment;
+ Become and stay connected with their followers;
+ Move strategically;
+ Avoid fads;
+ Nudge those holding a victim stance toward assuming responsibility for their own lives—a shift from reacting to creating;
+ Develop on-goingly the capacity to be a non-blaming (such internal judgments are kept to oneself), non-anxious (although such internal states may be present) leader; and
+ Experience sadness in those moments when they believe they must wisely choose inauthentic behaviors.

Peter not only discovers how to be an authentic leader but how to integrate authenticity in a business strategy which results in increased productivity. Though the story about

Peter is written as fiction, it is definitely not fantasy. It draws on my many years of successful experience with people like Peter in organizations.

Peter's journey—and yours—is that simple one back to the real you, the one-of-a-kind you who is peeking at these words behind the eyes of the adult you've become. That adult, the competent, business-like manager with sizeable responsibilities, may be pretty uneasy reading "this sentimental stuff about the real me," as one client put it a few years ago. To ease that discomfort, I offer the following companions for your journey:

"Except you become as a little child, you cannot enter the kingdom of heaven."

—*Jesus of Nazareth.*

"The question 'Who am I?' is meaningless to an infant. Instead, what shines through is awareness itself, the source of all wisdom."

—*Deepak Chopra.*

"The privilege of a lifetime is being who you are."

—*Joseph Campbell.*

"You are the unconditioned spirit trapped in conditions, like the sun in eclipse."

—*Rumi,* Persian poet.

"We spend our whole lives working back to the state of self-acceptance we were naturally born with."

—*Deepak Chopra.*

A good story about the issues presented in this chapter is *The Quest For Truth* in Part Four: Collected Short Stories.

◆◆◆

Part Four
Collected Short Stories:
Profiles in Authenticity

◆◆◆

Cultural Change in Organizations

Where's The Program?

Touring a manufacturing plant, a group of mid-career managers and executives was puzzled: In department after department they were met with stories of unprecedented success by unionized, hourly workers who talked (with no management present) about "before and after" conditions and results. The visitors reported being "deeply impressed" by these testimonials and wondered, "Before and after what?"

"We used to have 30 accidents a year. Now we've had 18 straight months without an incident," said a worker in a department that had previously averaged over 20 hours per week in forced overtime. Production demands are now being met with minimal overtime.

"We've had a few dozen grievances in the last four years. Before that, we averaged one a day!" said another. And in yet another shop, "Our budget was several million a year. Now we do nearly the same amount of equipment repair with an annual budget of about $500,000 [51] —and, yes, we order parts with VISA cards issued to us by the company. In addition, we now complete work orders in two to three days instead of two or three weeks."

It was clear that these employees were proud of their accomplishments and had a firm grasp on productivity figures and trends. The visitors could barely conceive of such a huge *decrease* in operating expenses for a department.

After the tour, the Human Resources Manager, a first-line supervisor and an hourly worker met with the tour group to discuss the visit. The guests included people with considerable experience (one a CEO, another from a larger manufacturing firm). As the visitors reflected one by one on their experience, the CEO seemed to sum up the most striking feature of their encounters in the plant: "They were so real!" he said. "Very straightforward. They just told it like it was."

What the visitors noticed was that the employees had not spoken from their roles but rather as one group of human beings to another, with no apparent hierarchy. The hourly worker John, who had been a change agent in the shop where the massive cost reduction had been achieved, joined the group to talk in more detail about the change. He hadn't used fancy charts and graphs, but instead he had simply (!) gone into the shop and said, "Hey, you guys, what's going on here?" From a stance of authenticity and respect, he helped them talk about issues, deal with their conflicts, and get excited about new ways to operate.

The CEO asked what kind of training was required to get these results. Paul, the first-line supervisor responded, "Most of the workers who spoke with you today had no special training. John, Bob, and I had a lot of training, for instance, in communication, conflict management, and coaching—all of these integrated with quality, safety and productivity goals."

"But didn't you have to re-train your entire work force?" the CEO exclaimed. He couldn't believe what he was hearing. "Something must have happened—they all spoke about 'before and after.'"

"No," Bob the HR Manager replied. "When a few key people start behaving authentically, it catches on with many others—not all, though. But we do work with groups/crews, like John did."

He continued, "'Before and after'? There's no name for it— no *program* name, no slogans—but everyone knows there's been a change."

The New Boss

He still remembers the first time he saw her. He couldn't believe it. Twenty-five years younger, and she was his new boss. Could've been his youngest daughter! He wondered why she was there. Sure, she had a degree, but Mike's degree was in living life and knowing more about this job than any man—or as he'd have to say now "any person"—alive.

She was wearing the steel-toed shoes, a hard hat, and safety glasses, and on her small frame the badges of position made her look like an alien who just stepped off a spaceship. "What does she know? What kind of b.s. will we have to put up with from her?" Mike wondered.

As she walked into the shop, her first sight was of a guy with a gray beard, wrinkled forehead, and stern face, about six feet tall, standing by some big equipment that she didn't recognize. She was scared stiff. Her hands trembled, and her mouth was dry. Was this, after all, a mistake? What was she doing here? Could she lead these guys? There's not one woman on this crew. Was she capable or unduly favored?

"Hi, I'm Jane." she said, calling up all the courage she could muster as she reached out to shake Mike's hand.

"I'm Mike, Mike Stansfield." This close to him, Jane could see that his eyes were blue, like her dad's, and she felt less frightened.

"Mike, I need your help. I'm told you're the senior employee here. Obviously I'm new, and I'm very nervous. I need support. Would you be my coach, my guide, at least until I get my feet on the ground?"

Mike was taken aback. Here was no brash young person trying to pretend she knew what she didn't know. It was an offer Mike couldn't refuse. Suddenly, he wanted her to succeed, like he would his own daughter.

Over the next months, he discovered that she was bright, well trained technically, and had a lot of spunk. It couldn't have been easy to take a job with this crew and then ask for help, Mike realized. Both were risky.

They ended up being great teammates. The other guys came along quickly, too. Jane knew more than they expected, was a fast learner, and would take a stand when necessary—no softy here. But she really got her authority to lead from three things:

1. She never pretended to know what she didn't.
2. She was a great learner—not only listening well, but encouraging the crew to teach her right on the factory floor.
3. When she disagreed, she did so gently but firmly. She never pretended that she knew for sure that her view was right, but rather she was clear that her job was to make certain (uncertain?) calls and not put off tough decisions.

Mike felt greatly respected by her and was sad when she took another position a few months later.

This morning the new boss arrived.

The first time he saw him, Mike couldn't believe his eyes! About thirty years younger with a fresh, young, boyish face. He looks like an alien in that hard hat, Mike thought, and what does he know, anyway? What kind of b.s. will we have to put up with?

Then Mike remembered the day Jane showed up at the plant, and he chuckled as he extended his hand to this *new* new boss.

"Hi, I'm Mike," he said.

"Hi, I'm Terry," the new guy replied.

"So, Terry, you can probably tell I'm an old-timer here. I'd like to show you around...help you get the lay of the land. What do you think?"

Terry's tentative grin expanded into a smile. "Thanks, Mike, you're just what the doctor ordered for the nervous indigestion I feel today. Whew, being the new boss just got a lot easier!"

Before and After . . . In A Non-Profit Agency

It wasn't long after I volunteered that I realized that most of the eighty-nine other volunteers were fictional. I asked my friend Mary, a new board member, "Where are the other volunteers? I don't see ninety. When I answered the appeal for volunteers, a staff member said there would be some training. But nobody knows anything about that either."

Mary was obviously troubled by my remarks. As she asked questions, informally and at the next two board meetings, she told me that she was beginning to feel like an unsuspecting player in a sinister mystery. For one thing, her initiatives to the agency staff seemed unwelcome. They treated questions more like a congressional probe than an honest inquiry. But Mary was stubborn, and she persisted.

What she discovered was that there weren't ninety volunteers, only about twenty-five, and some of them had no assignments. There had been plans for ninety, but somehow the recruitment activities had fallen short. And there had been plans for training, but no one had been adequately trained. Not even the twenty-five new volunteers.

I volunteered expecting to be assigned to either three or four disadvantaged clients (ranging from welfare moms to the elderly) or to work with veterans who met to talk about their life situations. But these preferences seemed to get lost in the shuffle of new assignments, changing priorities, and limited communication between staff and volunteers like myself.

In truth, the agency was a mess. The training director spoke eloquently about training events that rarely occurred but which indeed were budgeted! As the truth emerged about the failed recruitment and training activities, staff made excuses and blamed the dwindling number of volunteers for a lack of commitment.

But all that was B.C.—Before Charlotte, our new executive director arrived and gave us leadership like we've never had before!

Now? Now volunteers sign a contract. The first page is a commitment to a training program which includes actual experience with clients (or groups, if that's our focus) with self, peer, and staff assessments built in. It's a developmental training scheme where the less experienced like me get to observe and then assist with guidance until we're ready. Dates of trainings are included on the contract. There is a strong commitment to this training on the part of the staff.

The next page of the contract is signed by the director and key staff as they guarantee what they'll do for the volunteers. And the funding agencies receive a verifiable account of the work we do.

Now we have more volunteers than we can use! Professionals in the community give time and make their own commitments to help with the training. Our agency is seen as a place to both gain helping skills and be of service.

I'm proud that I spoke up despite the resulting hostility and denial by the staff. Mary remains on the board, having taken a leading roll in hiring Charlotte. And most of the old staff have been retained. It seems that when they finally got a real leader to direct the agency in an honest and caring way, they could make their own commitment to a productive workplace.

Volunteers will come out of the woodwork to join an agency where they can gain skills, really help people, feel deeply appreciated, and be held accountable. We want to be treated as professionals or, at least, aspiring professionals; and an agency that was serious, told the truth, and trained for competence would earn our loyalty.

This came to pass A.C.—After Charlotte. I still can't believe how much one person, leading in an authentic way, changed the agency. And, yes, I wasn't exactly passive myself. I didn't simply gripe to another volunteer—I took my concerns directly to someone who could act on them. So, Mary and I will take some kudos, too.

When I Back Off, They Break Records!

Following are excerpts of an interview conducted with a supervisor who had been with his company for thirty years. The interview was conducted after his crew's production had equaled the department record.

" I don't do it like I used to. When all this started, I couldn't imagine acting like I'm acting now.

"My 'rep'? They called me a 'tush hog.' You ever hunt wild boar? That was me. Now I'm Papo (paw-paw) which means 'Grandfather.'

"I had to learn to back off, but I was nervous about it. The first day I tried it, I went home about an hour after the swing shift began. I stayed by my home phone and pager. I told my wife, 'Can't take a walk today—I gotta stay for these calls.'

"No calls came.

"How'd they do? They broke records! I went in the next day, and they had broken the record for production! When I back off, they keep breaking records.

"I had to break my tough-guy pattern. Oh, I still get in that pattern now and then. I did it just yesterday. I started chewing out a guy and then I stopped myself. I said to myself 'I'm in my old pattern. Stop this.' I looked at him and said, 'I'm doing it again. Wait a minute. Joe, I'm sorry. Damn it. Let's start again. Tell me what happened, maybe I misunderstood.' So what I found out was that it really wasn't the way I thought—I *had* misunderstood!

"I couldn't have done this before *ToughStuff*™.[52] Funny, because after *ToughStuff*™ I didn't know what I had learned. I knew I'd been irritated, frustrated, and angry. But back at the shop I did things different.

"I knew I was smothering people with my old habits. I automatically started listening more. People had always told me to listen more, but I didn't. Now, after *ToughStuff*™ I was listening more. I knew the ship wouldn't sail if someone wasn't in charge, but I had to be the skipper in a different way. I know what I want, and they know what I want—where the plant is going and how our crew fits in. I still have to monitor work but without smothering. Like I said before, when I back off, they set records. My crew and I still disagree and sometimes outright quarrel, but I do it different now. I get out my point, and I truly listen. Both. That's what's really tough! But I do it now, here and more at home, and it works.

Besting The Best

When I graduated from Engineering School, I had a passion for designing, especially around technical processes that weren't working well. I was pleased when I got a job with a team of four which was assigned to a critical function affecting productivity.

They were very close to achieving world-class records with this process when I joined them, and after my first year we were matching the best done anywhere. But we were stuck. While we proudly maintained our record of achievement, another year passed by with no new improvements.

Then Dean Valdez, the new plant manager, arrived. He said to us, "You've done great! Now I want the efficiency improved by 15% in the next 12 months."

We were perplexed and told him so. "But our equipment is older...," we began, almost in chorus. He said, "Don't tell me why you can't do it. Tell me the problems and then tell me your strategy to achieve the 15%! Oh, and go see Merlin."

"Merlin? Who's he?" we asked.

"He's got the 15% up his sleeve," Valdez replied.

Well, we tracked down Art Merlin, and he did. He repeated Valdez's "You've done great" and then added, "Probably you've done all you can without help."

"Magic help?" we wondered.

"No, people help. The next gain in productivity will come when you seriously involve in your project the hourly employees who work with these processes every day."

We were resistant, but it didn't matter. The boss made it clear to us that we were to work closely with Merlin. Valdez listened to our resistance and even seemed empathetic about our concerns and then said, "I get it! You don't think a 15% gain is possible, and you don't think the hourly workers will help much. Right?"

"Right!" He finally understood.

Then he said a most astonishing thing: "You don't have to agree with me, but I want you to go for the 15% and, with Merlin's help, work with the hourly employees. Clear?" Yes, that was clear to all of us.

He continued, "Now if you're not willing to whole-heartedly do this, you are free to move to another engineering project. But I need everyone on *this* project to have their shoulder on the same wheel. Well...?"

Nobody left. I was surprised but pleased. I remember saying to myself, "This guy's really going to lead this company. He listens well but is obviously not going to run the company by majority vote or—worse yet—by minority veto." I said to him, "I'm with you, and I'm beginning to get excited."

After clarifying Merlin's role, Valdez left. The rest is history.

Once we got clear that we were "agents of change"—a very fancy way of saying that we were not bosses of the crews, Merlin worked with us and the crew bosses together. Expert knowledge, in my mind, had been the equivalent of telling people what to do. I was stunned by how much *they* knew. Once they got engaged, they were inventing ideas all day and into the night! And the "us *vs.* them" evaporated. We became a unit.

We more than achieved the 15% goal and did so more quickly than planned.

But most of all, I quit pretending. I began to say things like "I don't know" when I didn't or "Teach me about that" when someone else did. As the youngest of the two women on the team, I began to feel more respected and discovered that not pretending, being more my real self, felt pretty good. They, too, seemed eager to learn from me. The old game of "I'll show you how much I know!" was mostly gone.

Checks and Balances in Action[53]

My casual approach wasn't working. One of my oper-ators was performing in such a way as to cause signifi-cant lost production, not only in his furnace, but also on other furnaces in the system.

I had delegated the work, the "checks and balances" were in place, and I was receiving daily statistical reports. The problem was that the reports were confirming unacceptable work over a two-week period. Now, what do I do with the data? Oh, I knew the old way. Hit him over the head with it. But that doesn't work anymore—if it ever did. Sure, it may get results once. But in the long run I need to work *with* my people, not against them.

I tried a new strategy. Resisting my strong temptation to give the operator orders on the best way to solve the prob-lem, I instead asked him to talk to his colleagues about the ways they avoided these temperature drops. Specifically, I asked for an action plan, gave him a by-when, and said that I expected significant improvement or I would step in to solve the problem.

But I'm getting ahead of my story. It wasn't all that easy. When I first told him of my dissatisfaction with his perfor-mance, he became quite hostile. He ventilated loudly with several judgments about supervisors who were constantly pushing for more and more production even though they didn't know how to do the job.

What was different about me is that I recognized the "venting" as important and, one might say, as Act One in working out our conflict. So I didn't react—out loud, that is. Inwardly, my stomach was churning. I had already expressed my dissatisfaction. Now it was his turn. Someone said that if you let people vent for two minutes without interrupting, they'll be done. The problem is that most of us don't get our two minutes. He did. Also, while he was venting, I thought about what my reaction might have been if our roles were reversed. The same as his, I'll bet.

Then I acknowledged that he was very experienced in his work, and I expressed my confidence that he could raise his performance in this critical production area. I showed him the data. He acknowledged that the temperature drops "might be a little excessive." That's when I told him to come up with an improvement plan.

He did, and we won—both of us.

The data two weeks later was stunning. A statistical analysis indicated with a 95% confidence level that the improvement was due to the changes he made. I believe the improvement was a result of both my new way of relating to this employee and his response to me.

I have continued the monitoring and have been pleased to see that the improvements are long-lasting. The temperature drops for this operator are now consistent with other employees' performances. And there was another positive change as a result of this interaction. Our working relationship has improved. I complimented him on the change and asked, "What happened?" He started telling me different techniques that he had learned from other employees. It became obvious to me that he had, in fact, followed my suggestion to consult with his fellow employees. It has since become easier to discuss business topics with him, and our interactions are no longer confrontational.

Another change is an increase in my confidence about using statistical tools in the performance of my job. It gave me considerable satisfaction to make an intervention and later to have the data show that what I did made a difference.

Historically, the roles for supervisors at our company have been autocratic. Hourly employees were seldom given decision-making responsibilities. Now that there is a need to manage in a different way, hourly employees seem suspicious when we ask them to start making more decisions on their own.

Personally, I still find it easier to make decisions and tell others what to do. (My wife tells me that's what I do at home when all she wants is for me to listen.) Intellectually, I know that it is usually the least effective way to manage, so I struggle to move outside my comfort zone in order to be a more effective leader. At the same time, some hourly employees have become very comfortable with being told what to do. Consequently, a different style of leadership is sometimes uncomfortable to them as well.

But my goals are to:

+ Continue to push decision-making responsibilities to the lowest practical level.

+ View myself as a mentor, sponsoring, supporting and encouraging my employees to reach their highest potential.

+ Engage employees in discussions to help them understand the need for changes in the way we manage our processes and employees.

+ Challenge myself to look beyond my current comfort level to explore different ways to provide leadership.

+ Make sure, as I delegate more, that I have checks and balances in place so I can intervene when appropriate and in a way that respects my employees' experience, knowledge, and self-esteem.

I have learned that, while checks and balances are a critical component of delegating, they aren't enough! How I use the data is the leadership challenge for me.

See *Delegation*, page 143.

Cultural Change in Organizations

From Victim to Creator

For years I sat on my opinions. They would ask me to do stupid things, and I'd say, "OK." Other guys would do what they said and then, of course, have to do it over later. I don't like that—most don't. I'd try to figure out how to do it the best way without the boss knowing. We would joke about it, but, really, I hated it!

Then one day this joker started working with our crew and the boss. It's hard for me to call what he—we—did work because we were just sitting and talking. Well, he was good at getting everyone talking. He said we should talk about "what's working and what's not working." I told him that sitting here doing this crap wasn't working. His response stunned me. He definitely didn't argue. He said something like "Oh, yeah. I'm sure this must look like a huge waste of time, and I'll bet you're not the only one here who thinks that." Others agreed, and then we started talking about whether maybe anything would change as a result.

It wasn't until later that I realized how I was acting like a victim. I thought the success of these meetings depended on this new guy they called a " facilitator." I talked about whether "it" would work or not. I couldn't imagine that I had anything to do with the meeting. The meeting was an "it," and "they" were solely responsible for "its" success. That's sort of the way I thought about my work, too. Oh, some of it had to do with me but not much.

But now I see things differently. I say what I think—but in a new way. Now I tell people directly. If I think my boss has screwed up, I tell him instead of telling everyone else. And I tell him in a non-blaming way. Prior to some of the trainings we've had, I didn't know there was a non-blaming way to operate, and I didn't know how to be direct without insulting people.

OK, my boss and I raise our voices sometimes—hey, we get mad and frustrated—*but then we work it out.* He even calls me in to be the "facilitator" sometimes, working with him and one of my buddies when they are in a quarrel.

I'll tell you what's best. I do a lot of work on my own, and now I can do it without constantly asking for an OK about this or that. I have my own computer, I order my own materials. Oh, I use my boss occasionally when I get stuck, but otherwise, I move, man!

And now look at this—$130,000 in savings in one year! They haven't given me one red cent for it, but the new negotiations are supposed to correct that. Don't get me wrong—I want the money. And I should have it, not only for what I've saved the company but also for doing lots of things that the supervisor used to do. But you know what's most important? I love my work! I actually feel good when I walk in those gates each morning.

Oh, and that joker I mentioned? He turned out to be OK. I've learned how to do some of the stuff that he did. Now I know what it's like to be thought of as one of "them" from time-to-time—not great, but I can handle it.

The Quest for Truth

My business is truth! I can 't begin to tell you how many sermons I've delivered from the pulpit about honesty, authenticity, and accepting oneself even as the Source of Life accepts us. Then last summer I went to a Pastor's Conference where, instead of listening to lectures—about truth—we were in groups of twelve with two facilitators, learning how to *be* the truth.

The invitation from them was that we be authentic in the group. I could see that these leaders were really skilled. At first, I thought they were going to badger us to "spill our guts" or tell secrets about our personal lives, but they had no time or tolerance for that. When some of the group members—as you might expect—started talking *about* truth, the leaders had no tolerance for that, either. What else was there?

Over the next few hours in the group, it was sadly ironic to discover that we were a bunch of clergy who preached about truth but knew little about authenticity; we could talk about truth but we didn't know how to be it.

I recalled my favorite Kierkegaard quote: "The truth consists not in knowing the truth, but in *being* the truth." How do you *be* the truth? What is this "ministry" of authenticity and empathy—that is, what does it look like as I sit in a group with twelve people?

I struggled and resisted these ideas for a couple days, but eventually I began to realize how much I pretend. I have a front—a helping front—and even a certain tone of voice that I turn on in my ministerial role.

I don't want to be a role. I learned a lot that week and in subsequent work about the real me. I *am* OK. I do have fears. I sometimes get tired of helping. I'm beginning to realize that *I* am not the minister *role*. I don't have to pretend so much; pretending will ultimately be hazardous to my body, myself, and to my mission in life. I didn't become a pastor to play a role!

My journey to be authentic has been difficult. I'm learning about emotions that I've denied having most of my life. They're a part of me that I barely accept. And my authenticity comes out in awkward ways at times. I was troubled—really upset—recently by an ethnic joke told in my presence. I didn't laugh, and I was the only one who didn't. One person later told me that I shouldn't take life so seriously. Another said that "a man of the cloth" shouldn't get upset. Defending myself, I did remind him that Jesus turned over the tables in the temple and that Mohammed and Moses weren't exactly patsies!

Leading from an authentic place isn't easy. But my conversations with my parishioners are deeper now—more like I really want. I'm clearer about my goals for my ministry and for the parish. Who was it that said "The journey of a lifetime is being who you are"?

Cultural Change in Organizations

Appendices

Do You Really Want Change? [54]

Eleven Do's And Don'ts For Those Who Are Serious

1. Start With Yourself.

No matter how good you are, you will be caught up in some dysfunctional patterns. Whatever is not working now is being co-created by you. You are inevitably part of the dance. If you initiate change by fixing others, you'll be seen as a "do as I say, not as I do" sort of leader, cajoling others to straighten themselves out while continuing your own ineffective patterns. Don't blame the followers. Lead as a learner-leader. Quit dancing your part in the patterns you complain about. Lead with yourself.

Bottom Line: When things go wrong in your life, who's *always* there?

2. Energize And Focus From The Leader's Vision.

Yes, the leader's vision. While all employees must initiate and all managers must have a vision within the leader's vision, a body cannot function without a head. The true leader has a vision, is in touch with people, and stays the course for change against the inevitable resistance.

Bottom Line: Sail on a ship that has both a captain and a direction.

3. Don't Push an "Off-the-Shelf" Program.

Although the contents and packaging are usually slick, such programs often miss the mark, raise false expectations, reinforce the "flavor-of-the-month" mentality, and usually target "fixing the workers."

Bottom Line: Faddish programs are often demoralizing.

4. *Aim At Intact Work Groups.*

The change strategy cascades throughout the organization embracing all employees and enabling intact work groups (i.e., boss-employee groups) to enhance their effectiveness.

Bottom Line: If culture doesn't change at the work-group level, it doesn't change.

5. *Don't Ignore The Explosive Emergence Of Cross-Organizational Work.*

With the trend toward matrixed work where projects involve people from different work groups, serious attention must be given to planning and managing cross-functional tasks.

Bottom Line: In this age of telecommuting, the "matrixed organization" *can* be managed.

6. *Avoid the Self-Managed Consensus Trap.*

Encourage autonomy and clarity about authority. Without clear authority, there will be no autonomy. Decision-effectiveness requires appropriate influence by knowledgeable and experienced employees as well as gutsy decision-making by bosses who know how to manage. Good sports coaches know this blend.

Bottom Line: You can have both—clarity about authority and appropriate, energizing autonomy.

7. *Whatever The Change Is, Don't Name It–Do It!.*

Naming it is to polarize opinions about it. "I'm for it." "I'm against it." For or against what? According to whose interpretation?

Effective change is integral to the organization's direction and makes it easier to succeed. Effective change is not something more to do. Rather, it is a way to do what is essential more effectively. It is not a burden. It lifts the burden.

Bottom Line: Do the change. Be it.

8. *Don't Confuse Training With Change.*

Though organizational change may (and probably will) include training, that activity is a small part of success. Even then the training must not be packaged. It must be part of a strategy regarding who in the change process needs what particular training and when. Such training has to be sponsored by management—not HR, the Training Department, or Personnel.

Bottom Line: Think *change*, not training.

9. *Don't Hire Motivational Or Inspirational Consultants.*

People are already motivated. It is an insult to think that the problem lies in a lack of individual motivation. When leaders lead and change is managed as indicated here, people are motivated.

Bottom Line: Build it (the vision) and they will come.

10. *Integrate And Align The Change Process On All Fronts.*

Some companies are awash in various quality initiatives, leadership programs, and ways to measure and improve process performance. Assure that these are all integrated into one strategy that supports and is consistent with the leader's vision.

Bottom Line: Clarity. Alignment.

11. *Be Serious About Follow Up.*

In an organizational unit of five hundred people, there can be a significant culture shift in six months, including shifts from blaming to problem-solving; from decision-making confusion to clarity; from procrastination to decisiveness; from low trust to higher trust; and from confusion about accountability to clarity and acceptance of accountability. But most importantly *sustaining* the shift needs to be part of the change strategy.

Bottom Line: You are not serious about change *until* you are serious about follow up.

Peter's Change Strategy

- Set goals and state them clearly.
- Help direct reports get aligned with the goals and be open to feedback.
- Work closely with leaders of the union, hourly and salaried employees, to promote understanding of goals and plans.
- Communicate the goals across the organization in small groups with dialogue.
- Based on the goals set forth, expect the leaders of intact or cross-functional groups to sharpen goals for their units.
- Cascade a group process in each intact work group. Elements of the process must include clarity of goals, generation of issues and solutions, and follow up. (See page 136)
- Work with the company's most important cross functional (matrixed) projects. (Prior to the work, review pages 190-193)
- Develop a critical mass of strategic employees who have high interactive skills, that is, the capacity to take a stand, be decisive, stay the course against resistance, and stay connected.
- Develop a cadre of key people early in the process who will help sustain the shift in culture and the alignment around the leader's goals.

Peter was also well aware that he could easily turn this into a program—a new "flavor of the month"—rather than developing effective leadership therefore:

- He reviewed the *Eleven Do's And Don'ts For Those Who Are Serious* about change (Appendix A).
- He re-read Appendix C, "What It Takes To Pull Off A Cultural Change."

- He committed, in a new way, to follow up. Appendix A inspired Peter. He used number 11, *Be Serious About Follow Up*, as a catalyst to create a strategy that also incorporates pages 172-173, and 180-181. Then he held himself and his direct reports to these standards as well as instructing them to do the same throughout the entire organization.
- He reaffirmed the need to have skilled internal or external staff doing day-by-day nurturing until his cadre was developed. They would then take over the ongoing work of sustaining change, work that is constantly needed in a productive environment: dealing with conflict as it arises, making continuous contributions to work process improvement, ensuring decision clarity and role clarity, encouraging accurate data flow, and fostering authentic interaction.

What Does It Take
To Pull Off A Cultural Change?

❖ In an organization with 500 employees, an internal consultant with skills to guide a strategy like Peter's teamed with two external consultants for two years. The external consultants each spent 200 days supporting the leader's change strategy, especially steps 2, 6, 7, 8 and 9 (see Chapters 3 and 4). One of the external consultants worked closely with the plant manager.

Within twelve months there were dramatic changes in productivity and in the culture. The plant moved from the edge of survival to being a flagship for the industry and was referenced in a popular national business magazine for its 72% gain in productivity. Nine internal hourly and salaried employees were trained extensively to maintain the change and 40% of all employees were trained in the *ToughStuff*™ sequence similar to that described in Chapter 4.

❖ At an eighty-person software firm with no internal personnel skilled in implementing these strategies, several external consultants spent a total of about 120 days. Three employees attended an additional three-week training event. Thirty of the eighty employees were involved in *ToughStuff*™ training.

The company thrived, but with so many fortunate external factors occurring at the same time, it is difficult to demonstrate which gains were a result of the dramatic culture shift. Their key software program was produced on schedule for the first time. A mix of hard and soft data[55] support that change did occur in areas such as the following:

♦ Clarity about jobs, goals, decision-making and the authority to act

- Alignment throughout the organization
- Ability to deal with conflict
- Job satisfaction
- Movement from blaming to "make-it-happen"
- Production schedules met or exceeded
- Achievement of business objectives

Also, another software firm completed its major software product on schedule, for the first time. All of the components of successful cross-functional work (as in Peter's strategy) had been intensively coached by the consultants.

❖ Firms or departments of various sizes have successfully pulled off and sustained the culture shift described in this book. Those that sustain the shift invest in training employees, including top management and hourly employees in the skills necessary for the change work as described in this book. These people then bring authentic leadership to the workplace each day and, by doing so, are a driving force behind clarity, decisiveness and accountability. They are skilled in the processes described here. They are aligned with the organization's direction and constantly pay attention to safety, cost, quality, and the appropriate involvement and influence of all employees. Their task is simple and unchanging:

- Lead with yourself, authentically
- Stay connected with people
- Encourage and reward initiative
- Deal with conflict productively
- Encourage the movement towards less supervising and towards more delegation with clear checks and balances
- Notice and help fix what has to be fixed
- Coach...train...coach...train...be!

But sometimes the vitality drains away. Sometimes the shift isn't sustained even if the company starts losing money, and employees become demoralized. Of course, a critical factor is the arrival of a new top boss. Often this new boss has little understanding about the key(s) to the previous success. Perhaps they are so technically oriented that they think the success must have been primarily due to technical expertise! Perhaps they see people involvement as "fluffy" or as "touchy-feely" and of little value.

Or the reverse is often true. That is, they are so permissive that they don't lead and soon the organization is being run by the strongest and toughest mid-managers with no leadership from the top. In my experience, this is the primary cause of decline.

Cultural Change in Organizations

Organizational Culture Shifts

A culture shifts when these factors move from left to right

From	Toward
Focus on Blaming	➤ Focus on making it work
Language of "I'll try"	➤ Language of "I'll do it"
Poor follow-through on plans	➤ High implementation reliability
Low trust	➤ High trust
Poor safety record	➤ Excellent safety record
Firefighting	➤ Root-cause solutions
People who use and repair have no input on equipment purchase	➤ The people who use and repair have input prior to decision being made
No by-whens (clear completion dates)	➤ By-whens in place and working
No rewards or consequences	➤ Effective reinforcement and reprimands
No clear accountability	➤ Single-point (not a group) of accountability is in place
Little influence by workforce	➤ Appropriate influence by all levels
Decision making is unclear	➤ Who decides what is clear
Shoot the messenger	➤ Honor the messenger even if the message is difficult to hear
Conflicts are avoided	➤ Conflicts are faced constructively
Conflicts are handled in an authoritarian way	➤ Handled in a direct and problem solving way
Not able to get materials or information when needed	➤ Able to get these when needed

1	2	3	4	5	6	7	8	9	10
LOW									HIGH

The scales, and variations thereof, have proven time and again to be a reliable catalyst for shifting workplace culture. The questions themselves lend clarity to the desired future state, but it is the process of engaging employees in dialogue and action, described below, which is the key to moving towards a more productive culture.

A consistent gain of 3 to 4 points can be expected in a few months when the change strategy includes a well-managed group process engaging each intact workgroup throughout your organization. This means each intact work group scores the data based on how they think it is in their immediate work group. If they must support or be supported by others outside their group they keep that in mind as they do their scoring. The group then studies their data and decides which areas need improvement. From here they clarify specific examples of the issues that led to their scores and begin to suggest ways to improve them. They do this with input from all but keeping in mind that the boss has the *responsibility* and *authority* to name specific improvements needed or problems that must be addressed if they are missing in the discussion. Through this dialogue the group creates specific actions for improvement that include who will do what and by when. Finally, there must be periodic follow through where progress is rated and new plans are developed as needed.

Improvement on these items means higher quality, productivity, and safety.

For instance, the initial data taken in one organization I worked in showed that the highest scoring group (of 8 groups) had 2% of the safety incidents in the previous 12 months and the lowest scoring group had 28%. Absenteeism was twice as high in the lowest group; productivity and quality were also the lowest. After following the processes in this book, that organization had a 72% productivity gain as referenced in Business Week June 1993.

Delegation[56]

Delegation is obviously not new. However, there are some traps that frequently derail its effectiveness. The most common is to delegate without clear boundaries and/or expectations about how to monitor the work. Out of sight and mind does not mean a lack of accountability. The questions below are intended to help you appropriately delegate authority in order to create a faster and more effective organization. They provide a methodical way to put in appropriate checks and balances. Delegation without due diligence to these questions is more accurately called abdication and could lead to lack of clarity, poor results, and no quality control.

1. What is the task or new decision accountability?
2. Is the employee ready now or do you need to get them ready?
   - If no, what training do they need?
3. What are the parameters?
   - Within what boundaries can they operate?
4. If things go wrong what are they to do?
   - When do they call you for help?
   - When and under what conditions are they to call any resource for help?
5. Do they know how it fits into the greater system?
   - If no, explain how it fits?
6. How will it be monitored?
   - The intention of this stage is to have a dialogue between you and your employee to develop a monitoring system that both a) provides the information that you need and, b) is simple. How often you are updated is based on the experience of your worker.

Delegation is both art and science. Choosing what and when to delegate is the art. Gaining specificity on the task components and monitoring system is the science. The responsibility to monitor the work is yours. However, the responsibility to keep you informed is the employees. Therefore, the employee should be involved in developing the monitoring system. An effective strategy is to have them develop the system and share it with you for approval. The aim is to create a system that is easy for the employee and provides you with the required information.

Delegation is a process-not an end state. If used well you will create a workplace that moves fast, significantly engages its employees, and reaches or exceeds its bottom line goals. The paradox of delegation is that in order to gain control you must push some decision authority closer to your employees. The process we have outlined is intended to help you do that in a methodical way that avoids the extreme of delegation which is abdication. Without effective monitoring of the delegated work you risk losing touch with your workers and having them inadvertently move the business in a direction that ultimately could hurt the bottom line.

See *Checks and Balances in Action*, page 119.

Culture Can Be Built:
PECO Nuclear Turn Around[57]

by Gilmore Crosby

I n 1987 the Nuclear Regulatory Commission (NRC) shutdown Peach Bottom Atomic Station (PBAPS) due to human performance issues. When the Philadelphia Electric Company (PECO) began rebuilding their Nuclear organization, they happened upon Robert P. Crosby, one of a legion of resources brought to bear on the organization. Crosby began applying the same techniques he had been honing since the 1950s. His prior experience with DOE and Rancho Seco Nuclear helped open the door. At Rancho Seco he crafted a turnaround on an MOV project that was months behind schedule (unfortunately, that effort and additional culture change work was wasted when the public voted to shut down the site permanently). At PECO, Crosby influenced the extensive organizational development activity that took place in the wake of the shutdown. This special edition of Human Factors explores Crosby's methods, which have been replicated in numerous organizations, and continue to be utilized today.

On March 31, 1987 Peach Bottom Atomic Power Station was indefinitely shutdown, following a series of human performance and equipment related incidents. Infamously, operators were found sleeping on the job, playing video games, engaging in rubber band and paper ball fights, and reading unauthorized material.

As if in anticipation of the Institute of Nuclear Power Operators (INPO) yet to be developed human performance model, blame was not simply placed on the operators. "Latent organizational weakness" was targeted by industry experts and regulators alike. INPO President Zack Pate came to the unprecedented conclusion that, "Major changes in the corporate culture at PECO are required." In September of 1988 NRC Chairman Lando Zech told senior management officials of PECO, "Your operators certainly made mistakes, no question about that. Your corporate management problems are just as serious." By April 1988 this unusual emphasis on mismanagement contributed to the President of PECO resigning and the retirement of the CEO.

By 1996 both Limerick and Peach Bottom were designated excellent by INPO, and given strong Systematic Assessment of Licensee Performance (SALP) ratings by the NRC. Many factors contributed to this stunning success story. The following are the key organizational development strategies that were employed:

1. **Clarify Goals and Build Alignment.** Management must lead and communicate. They must set clear goals, such as increased capacity factor and lower costs, and lead towards them. They must continually communicate the goals, and engage the organization to as to understand, monitor, and support efforts to achieve the goals.

2. **Develop a Critical Mass of Employees with High Interactive Skills.** On the other hand, setting clear goals without developing the organization is as likely to backfire as not. The Clinton Significant Event Report (SER), for example, pointed out that goal alignment was actually part of the problem leading to the 1996 incident at that station. The SER cites management emphases on the need to "maximize plant capacity factors and minimize forced outage rate" as an underlying cause...goals which are shared by every nuclear plant in the nation.

   Such goals need to be balanced with a carefully reinforced emphasis on conservative decision making and surfacing of issues. A culture of openness must be fostered or vital information will stay underground. To this end, a critical mass of employees at all levels of the organization must work on their leadership skills. This learning must be experiential and not just standard classroom, and be reinforced in subsequent live work interactions.

The behavioral skill set should include an increased capacity to foster a productive nuclear safety environment by giving clear direction, taking a stand for what you believe in, holding yourself and others accountable, fostering communication up and down the hierarchy, managing conflict, connecting with emotional intelligence to all levels of the organization, and continually developing yourself, others, and the organization.

Without intentional on-going development, complacency results. *This is especially true of successful organizations!* All individuals and organizations have blind spots. As the Clinton VP put it: "We believe complacency played an important part in our performance decline. We thought we had established all the programs and practices necessary to be a top performing plant."

3. **Cascade Goal Alignment and Continuous Improvement Conversations in all Intact Teams.** Renew on a regular basis. Every team should stop periodically to assess how it's functioning. Bosses and subordinates need honest feedback from each other, and the entire group needs to strategize on how to improve their work within the context of the organization's goals. This should be an expectation, with guidelines, not just a "nice to do" which is done any which way.

Crosby's strategy of work group continuous improvement was sustained for years at PECO Nuclear through a unique survey-feedback process, and through new reporting relationship (NRR) meetings. The survey process allowed each intact work group to see their own data, derive their own conclusions, and develop solutions to problems within their own sphere of influence. The NRR meetings occurred at all levels. They served the dual purpose of supporting a smooth transition whenever a leadership change occurred, and of seizing continuous improvement opportunities during the change.

4. **Drive Cultural Change through Key Cross-Functional Projects.** At PECO Nuclear this was done through changing the approach to outages. Change doesn't come through training (although training can support change). Change the organization by implementing desired behaviors in the context of key initiatives. Outage execution, for example, is an excellent time to reinforce single point accountability, conservative decision making, conflict resolution skills, surfacing of issues, and related behaviors.

5. **Create a cadre of key line people early in the process who can help facilitate the change.** At PECO Nuclear many of these people rose through the ranks in the organization, including the current VP at Limerick. These people, craft as well as manager personnel at PECO Nuclear, must have all of high interactive skills mentioned above. At Peach Bottom, they were woven into every initiative, and provided the following on a formal and informal basis:

   ◆ Individual coaching regarding conflict, communication skills, etc.
   ◆ Third party conflict resolution
   ◆ Meeting design and/or facilitation
   ◆ Survey feedback and NRR facilitation

In short, the transformation of PECO Nuclear was no fluke. Many variables came together, including great personnel and a unique burning platform. Nonetheless, the organizational development approach described above was a critical enabler, and continues to be implemented in nuclear and non-nuclear organizations to this day.

Under-Functioning: It's Role in the Sponsor Agent Target Advocate Theory

by Chris Crosby

In 1992, Dr. Darryl Conner published his famous book titled "Managing at the Speed of Change[58]," which is about managing in fast-moving organizations. The book outlines his theory of change called Sponsor Agent Target Advocate (SATA). SATA highlights key roles around daily tasks, projects or changes that are both universal to all organizations and critical for success. The roles are:

♦ The **Sponsor** (*initiating* or *sustaining*), who legitimizes the change or work

♦ The **Change Agent**, who facilitates the change or work

♦ The **Advocate**, who has an idea or wants things to be different

♦ The **Target**, who carries it out

No matter what official role or function you play in an organization, you are also in at least one SATA role, which has specific behaviors needed for successful work, projects or change. The dilemma of course, is that the majority of us are unaware of the SATA roles we are in and are thus unsure of how to leverage those roles for success.

That same year, Robert P. Crosby published his book titled "Walking the Empowerment Tightrope[59]." In it he acknowledges Dr. Conner for his work on SATA and adds a critical distinction without which SATA cannot be fully understood. Crosby's unique theory of authority in systems adds clarity about the role of the Sponsor – specifically, that **you can only "sponsor" your direct reports**. Often, unproductive work and failed change efforts are a result of the lack of understanding of this critical distinction.

In 1994 Crosby published "Solving the Cross-Work Puzzle[60]," a book about how to manage projects and survive in a cross functional workplace. In it he emphasizes two critical types of Sponsors, sustaining and initiating. The initiating Sponsor is a single person above all people who must do the task, project or major change, while the sustaining Sponsor is the direct supervisor of the Target. These two books by Crosby highlight the importance of building sponsorship at the sustaining Sponsor level.

SATA, with Crosby's adaptation, has influenced everything I do as an organizational development consultant over my 15-plus years of practice. Using SATA to chart out a problem or dilemma has proven to be an important analysis tool in building strategies for success. In SATA terms, I have lived my professional life in the role of a Change Agent with no authority over anyone with whom I am working. What I *do* have is lots of influence through technical, interpersonal and referent means. ("Referent" is the word-of-mouth stories told about you.)

As a Change Agent, I have always been heavily influence by SATA and the concept of "over-functioning." Essentially, over-functioning is when you, without having authority, tell others that they *have to* do what you say. It is acting as if you are boss when you really aren't.

Over-functioning happens all the time and creates all sorts of problems in organizations. Its dangers have always been taught as a core part of SATA.

During my years of internal and external consulting, I began to notice a pattern in organizations beyond what is traditionally taught in SATA. Over-functioning helps explain some aspects of how systems get stuck with unclear and confused authority; yet it misses other aspects. Many people allow things to slip or go unnoticed. These employees are acting under the real authority they are expected to take (whether clarified or not).

Not stepping up and taking appropriate authority adds a critical piece as to why tasks don't get done, projects slip and changes fail. **I call this behavior "*under*-functioning," as it amounts to letting things slide.** Here are some examples of how under-functioning has impacted some fairly common work situations:

♦ A Change Agent in the role of project manager cancelled a scheduled follow-up meeting (without consultation with the boss of those in the meeting) because "he didn't want to bother people" despite the fact that the project was worth millions and the boss wanted it to happen.

♦ A Sponsor didn't want to have his longtime employee be the project manager for a multimillion-dollar project, so, instead, he had three people co-lead the project. He did this in order to avoid "hurting feelings," even though having three people co-leading is dysfunctional and increases the odds of battles over direction.

♦ A Target/Advocate who didn't raise a problem with his supervisor because "he didn't want to bother the boss" even though the issue was critical to getting production back up and running.

I believe *under*-functioning happens more often in organizations than over-functioning, and it results in work not getting done, projects slipping, deadlines being missed and millions of dollars being lost. Based on this belief, I now teach under-functioning as a standard part of SATA. Moreover, under-functioning also helps explain behavior for all SATA roles.

Here are some common ways under-functioning shows up for each role:

Sponsors: *Feather Ruffling Avoidance*
Whenever a tough conversation needs to happen but doesn't—or clear authority is not put in place—because of fear of upsetting someone, and it results in compromises in completion of work, decisions or slipped timelines.

Change Agents: *Letting Timelines, Meetings and Tasks Slip*

Any time a task, timeline or meeting is allowed to slide without a conscious choice by the sustaining Sponsor who must make sure that work is balanced between the short- and long-term functioning of the business.

Advocates/Targets/Change Agents: *Holding Issues*

Whenever an employee is aware of a critical issue yet does not tell their sponsor so that it remains unresolved, and it results in work not being completed or quality being compromised.

Any SATA Role: *Conflict Avoidance*

Any time more than one person or group has differences with each other that, if left unresolved, will likely mean work will not get completed on time and with quality.

Of course, this is not an exact science. They key question here is, "Does the business potentially suffer because of this behavior?" And yes, there are other systemic, individual and interpersonal issues at play that help create the above dynamics. Humans often have a hard time with conflict, including listening and receiving difficult information, and there is a tendency to want to tread lightly on others' emotions which is appropriate at times but detrimental at others. All these and more help increase under-functioning in businesses.

Since it is clearly happening in most organizations, the question becomes "What can be done about it?" The answers to that question are many, and they range from total culture change to one-on-one coaching. Using SATA as a model is a good starting place to set clear expectations of all SATA roles through dialogue with the sustaining Sponsor(s) and all key players about what to do if the above mentioned behaviors arise.

Under-functioning in organizations is as old as the hills, and *unconscious* under-functioning is responsible for high amounts of waste in organizations. My excitement comes from the identification of its existence in a way that adds clarity to how to manage it.

My hope is that, by increasing awareness of under-functioning, organizations will be able to develop better strategies for reducing its impact.

Results: Organizational and Personal Health

"**F**olk-wise" managers and employees know that a healthy environment as envisioned by Peter in Chapter Two contributes to personal, emotional ("employee morale"), and physical health (accidents, back pain, headaches, and so forth) as well as productivity and quality. Research results confirm this common wisdom.

Here's a selection of results from our history:

+ A light manufacturing firm saw:
  ...absenteeism drop 40%,
  ...industrial accidents drop 21%, and
  ...worker's compensation claims drop 29%,
  ...while sales increased 23%.
+ A fast food chain saw employee turnover cut in half.
+ A printing establishment
  ... reduced its wasted materials from 11.2% to 1.5%
  ...while reducing lost labor (due to illness, accidents, and unknown causes) from 17.6% to 2.8%.
+ A heavy industry recorded that the crew with the best productivity and quality record had
  ...one-half the absenteeism,
  ...one-thirteenth the number of safety incidents, and
  ...the best score on a supervisor/employee relationship survey
  as compared with its lowest performing crew.
+ A high-tech department of 85 employees went from 22 grievances to 0.
+ A heavy industry department of nearly 1000 employees went from 200 grievances in one year to 17 in the next, while productivity increased.

♦ Work authorizations written and completed in a high-tech firm more than tripled one year to the next while safety violations in that same period dropped to an all-time low and productivity multiplied.

Why Successful Practices Become "Fads" And Fade Away[61]

Organizations have spent billions of dollars attempting to replicate practices with occasional success, but many have failed. Such new programs often are based on a successful practice but fail in the new application, making way for the next quick fix.

Most employees can remember one or another new program imposed by management, insisting that everyone follow the same practice. And most employees also remember how many such efforts (quality initiatives, new business systems) failed to take hold. They call such failed attempts "fads" or "flavor of the month" programs.

Why do they fail and what creates success in disseminating good practices so that results are achieved? First, let's review two extremes that guarantee failure.

Become a true believer in the practice and push it on everyone. This is the most popular implementation method. Companies spend mega-bucks on "cookie-cutter" approaches, and training companies flourish by marketing such packages. CEOs often forget the wisdom about managing for results, not for "activities." They count activities—how many people attend quality training or how many crews are now "self-directed"—rather than looking at the results of such trainings or new practices in the key areas of safely, cost, and quality.

In this extreme, experts on the particular methodology or program being implemented are dispatched to convince, coerce, or otherwise manipulate the resisting parties into conforming to the new approach. And even if the top executive has mandated the change, there is intense resistance and sabotage of the essentials in the new method.

Let the employees decide whether they want to adopt the new program. In the other failure scenario, the new practice is suggested and left for individual or group discretion. A few adopt it, some adapt it to fit their needs, and many ignore it. There is a better way. The key is in the difference between the words "adopt" and "adapt"—

> Adopt = Swallow it whole
>
> Adapt = Fit it to your needs

—and in the paradoxical blending of these two in a unified construct.

Here are some fundamental principles and steps in the sharing of successful practices:

1. The successful practice must be presented, warts and all, as it is practiced. The presenters of this knowledge are instructed not to generalize to other situations, not attempt to apply it for the audience, and not sell it. Rather, they are to share accurate data with genuine enthusiasm but no exhortations ("This is the greatest thing since sliced bread!") or admonitions ("You must do this or lose market share!").

2. As clearly as possible, measurable outcomes—for which all will be accountable— should be identified and communicated by the sponsoring executives. People will be held accountable for successful results and not whether they exactly replicate the method.

3. Those receiving the knowledge about the successful practice need to demonstrate their ability to articulate accurately the original practice. No arguing. Rather, repeat back the words and paraphrase the meanings (i.e., "Here is what I heard you say, and I'm translating it into the following meanings. Do my meanings match yours?").

4. The receivers derive implications for their unique situation. Temporarily accepting the validity of the successful practice, they consider what it would take to implement it at their location in their unique way.

5. The initiating executive or key manager, perhaps in the midst of step four, clarifies those aspects, if any,

of the practice that are so central that they are not negotiable. Thus, the receivers have clarity about what is to be adopted and what can be adapted. While still striving for results and not activities as the goal, the executive may have compelling reasons (e.g., standardizing purchasing of costly equipment) for "edicting" certain core elements. That which is to be adopted will be met by resistance, of course, which leads to the next step.

6. The initiating executive must then listen, stay firm about the core, respect disagreement, and respect anger or frustration if it surfaces. After appropriate airing, s/he should again state the core (which may have shifted slightly—but genuinely, not as the result of placating but of careful listening) and then state the firm expectation that people will follow the leader!

7. The completion of the work includes the selection of practices to be adapted, the sequencing of these, and the planning for additional training or resources needed to implement both the adopted and the adapted practices.

Successful transfer of knowledge is enhanced by a clear attention to the adoption/ adaptation distinction. Ideally, one should minimize adoption and maximize adaptation, while keeping one's eye on results, not methods. Adaptation is a natural process. This is true because situations where new practices are to be implemented are unique; because the communication of a complex practice is almost certain to be misunderstood; because humans are most motivated when they use their own creative juices; and because a key ingredient in a new process or practice is the involvement and belief in the process by those who will, day by day, carry out the practice.

Cultural Change in Organizations

How to Effectively Manage Transitions in Leadership and Key Personnel [62]

by Gilmore Crosby

A PRACTICAL METHODOLOGY

O ne of our readers recently requested advice from *Human Factors* on how to manage changes in key personnel; in his case a change of personnel in a key supplier organization. This issue focuses on a simple method for managing such changes: transition meetings/new reporting relationship meetings (NRRs).

NRRs were developed by the U.S. Navy (and have been practiced for decades by Crosby & Associates). The Navy conducted research on the impact of transitions (see Chart #1, "Characteristics of the Transition State"), and documented a consistent decrease in effectiveness and produc-

CHART #1:
CHARACTERISTICS OF THE TRANSITION STATE

1. High uncertainty/low stability.
2. High levels of "inconsistency" (perceptual).
3. High emotional stress on people.
4. High energy (often undirected).
5. Control becomes a major issue.
6. Past patterns of behavior become explicitly valued.
7. Conflict increases, especially intergroup.
8. Productivity decrease.
9. Transition is an error-likely situation (miscommunication, mistakes and injuries are more likely to occur).*

* This item added by the editor based on the human performance fundamentals work conducted during recent years by the nuclear industry.

tivity lasting approximately six months (Chart #2, below). Their findings further show a reliable reduction of the period of disruption from six months to a month when the NRR method was applied.

CHART #2: THE TRANSITION STATE

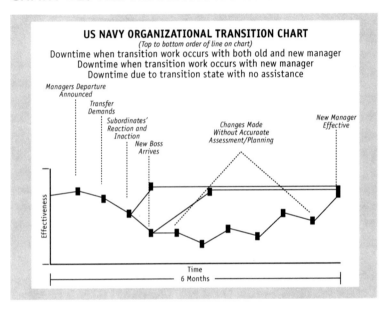

US NAVY ORGANIZATIONAL TRANSITION CHART
(Top to bottom order of line on chart)
Downtime when transition work occurs with both old and new manager
Downtime when transition work occurs with new manager
Downtime due to transition state with no assistance

Managers Departure Announced

Transfer Demands

Subordinates' Reaction and Inaction

New Boss Arrives

Changes Made Without Accuraate Assessment/Planning

New Manager Effective

Effectiveness

Time
6 Months

The essence of an NRR is a facilitated conversation between the subordinates and new leader as soon as possible (or the continuing personnel and the new key person which, for the sake of brevity, we will refer to as the "subordinates" and the "leader" throughout the remainder of this document). Although many leaders assume some time should pass before such a session, no period of familiarization is necessary prior to an NRR. The Navy conducted their NRRs as soon as the new officer came aboard.

An NRR does, however, involve preparation. At minimum, the facilitator interviews the new leader prior to the session. Ideally, they interview the subordinates as well. The interviews allow the facilitator an opportunity to build rapport, discuss the process, clarify their own role (which is to orchestrate the process and reinforce active listening skills on the part of the leader and the subordinates), and stimulate the participants thinking. Topics range from the leader's intentions regarding decision making and leadership style to the subordinates' views on the organization's strengths and weaknesses.

The NRR session begins with introductions, any expectations the new leader may have (such as inviting people to be as open with them as possible), the facilitator's role, a "ground-rule" for the dialogue (to be elaborated on later in the...article), and a review of the agenda. It's also helpful if the new leader gives a brief overview of how they intend to manage, so the participants have more to chew on.

The new leader then steps out of the room for approximately an hour, giving the participants a chance to think out loud and get organized. A cheat sheet of what individuals want to ask or tell the leader is recorded on a flipchart. The facilitator assists the participants in getting behaviorally specific. For example, if they want the new leader to "trust" them, or "show respect," the facilitator will ask them to clarify *what behaviors* would lead them to that judgment about the leader (the subordinates might, for instance, believe delegating certain decisions and tasks would be evidence of trust and respect).

When working on a cross-functional relationship (such as the change in a key supplier position that prompted this article) modifications to the process, such as having both parties identify what they can do different to improve the work flow, can help get the relationship off on the right foot.

The leader's return is our cue to elaborate on the "ground-rule" (as promised above): the design calls for individuals to *speak for themselves* when it's time for their items on the cheat sheet. The outcome of many team members gaining the experience of testing the waters directly with the new boss (and visa versa) will be watered down if the facilitator or a spokesperson speaks for them, or if the boss reads off the questions and launches into a monologue. If a participant doesn't want to risk being direct during the meeting, the facilitator encourages them to find some timely way *outside the NRR* to raise it with the leader. Because it can initially invoke some anxiety, it's important to discuss this ground-rule in the preparation interviews, and again at the start of the session.

During the dialogue the facilitator tracks commitments (who, what & by-when...tasks and behaviors agreed on by the leader and/or the subordinates), helps untangle miscommunication, and continues to reinforce "being direct." The process is complete with the exhaustion of the "ask/tell" list. For maximum effect, commitments are reviewed in a similar session 1 to 3 months down the road, and informally during the interim.

CHART #3: NRR SAMPLE AGENDA

1. Supervisor kickoff/agenda/ground rules/leader's expectations/leadership style
   (30 minutes maximum).
2. Supervisor exit & group generates ask/tell list
   (approx. 1 hour).
3. Group dialogue/agreements
   (two hours if briskly paced).

The following questions are intended to be used in the new reporting relationship meeting.

Potential Transition Topics

by Chris Crosby

The following represent common areas to be addressed during work transitions. They are meant to stimulate thinking of what could be brought up during this meeting.

CREDENTIALS

- What is your background? What skills and knowledge do you bring? What degrees/education do you have?
- What do you want us to know about you?
- Do you tend to more hands on or hands off?
- What type of behavior is necessary to be effective while working with you?

BASIC COMMUNICATION AND POLICIES

- How do you like to be communicated with? By email? In person? By phone?
- Do you hold work team meetings? How often? Past meetings were *effective/not effective.*
- How do you want to handle vacations?

SOLVING ISSUE/PROBLEMS

- If I have a problem how much data do you need? How would you prefer to receive it?
- Can I bring you issues that I do not know how to solve?

STRUCTURE

- How are decisions made? Who is consulted before the decision? Who is informed after the fact? Who can veto a decision?

- I can/cannot make decisions that I need to do my job.
- There are a few decisions that I have to wait for in which I would like to make myself.
- Our work flow is *working/not working.*

CURRENT ISSUES

- Our work group has been running at X efficiency.
- The major issues are X and Y.
- These are the organization's key strengths? Weaknesses?
- These things get in the way of me doing my job.
- How do you function as a team? What is your role in the team?
- I hope you change this part of our culture.

WORK TEAM INPUT NEEDS

- As a team we *get/don't* get tools/info/support to do our job.
- Our internal suppliers/customers work *well/poorly.*

EMPLOYEE UTILIZATION

- I have X skills that are not being utilized
- Our department is structured *effectively/not effectively.*
- Person task fit is working *well/not* working well in our job.

HISTORY

- I want to conserve *this part/none* of how we were functioning prior to your arrival
- Life here has been *easy/difficult.* Here is the story of the last ten years.
- These are the informal rules that determine how things really get done here.

DIFFICULT MOMENTS OF DISAGREEMENT (CONFLICT)

+ How would you describe your conflict style?
+ If I disagree with you can I tell you? In public? Behind closed doors?

ACCOUNTABILITY

+ How do you hold your people accountable?
+ Our past boss *always/never/rarely* supported new initiatives or critical daily work by gaining clarity of direction and holding people appropriately accountable.
+ There is/isn't singlepoint accountability for each role, task and action.
+ Actions here *always/never/rarely* get done on time and when slipping people *always/never/rarely* let others know when they will miss the date.

Succeeding With "Troubled" Employees

"Troubled" here refers to an employee who may lose their job. But don't read further if you have identified a "troubled" employee whom you are convinced is technically unable to succeed or whom you truly don't want to succeed.

Also, stop reading if you are not willing to see this as, potentially, a *systems* rather than *personality* problem. Translated, this means that you may be a part of the problem. That is, you may have a troubled work system relationship on your hands rather than a troubled employee problem. Still reading? Then explore this illustration.

Among the mechanics in your shop, it's very clear that Mike is viewed as a problem employee. Dealing with Mike directly presents you with the following possibilities:

Option A: Bring Mike in for a talk, making it clear what Mike must and must not do for his work to be considered satisfactory. Initiate some disciplinary procedures so he gets the message that you mean business.

Option B: Meet with the group to find out what's going well and what's not going well. Specifically, explore whether people get the information and materials they need to do a good job and whether they have the authority they need. Find how clear they are about their tasks and priorities and if they are able to significantly influence the purchase and repair of equipment, materials, and other resources needed to do their job.

Of course, Option B was the system option. If Option A is your usual pattern, then you may be caught up in the 20th Century culture of individual psychological motivation. If so, it is highly unlikely that your efforts to boost productivity, quality, and morale will achieve the level of success which you and your work group want.[63]

HOW SYSTEMS PROBLEMS CREATE POOR PERFORMANCE

In research data gathered from over 600 companies, organizational factors were isolated that lead to stress. Key factors include:

1. Lack of authority to do what I'm given responsibility for;
2. Lack of clarity about my role;
3. Lack of clarity about my role on the part of others (thus my boundaries are constantly tested);
4. Lack of specificity in performance evaluation or feedback;
5. My lack of understanding of the larger picture about where my department and company are going;
6. My sense of not being appreciated for work well done; and
7. My lack of influence over those things that affect my work and around which I have talents, experience, and expertise.

It's ironic that managers spend untold hours on so-called "troubled employees" rather than deal with systemic issues that create a stressful environment. An hourly worker in a manufacturing plant reported that his department had dropped from 200 grievances a year to about 30 when systemic approaches and improved day-to-day conflict skills were initiated.

Now I'm assuming that you've solved the systems dilemma and still think it's a troubled employee issue. OK. From here it's simple. Just follow the process that starts on the next page. Caution: If you do it well, the employee will succeed nine times out of ten. For the tenth, you'll have the documentation to do whatever is within the authority granted you by your organization and its policies.

Examples of Not Being Specific about relational goals		Examples of Specifics by Two Supervisors Demonstrating different interpretations and their own unique expectations
Take more initiative.	*May mean*	"Come into my office almost every day with fresh ideas to explore."
	Or may mean	"Come back in a month and tell me what you've done."
Be cooperative.	*May mean*	"Tell your peer-workers what you have been doing and request their input."
	Or may mean	"Don't bug peers with your project unless asked."[64]

I. Clarify your expectations

A. Write down your expectations. Be specific about what you want technically and relationally.

B. Share the rough draft of your expectations with a neutral third party[65] who can help you translate all judgmental words into specifics.

II. Inform your employee:

Meet with your employee to set up the process for improvement. Be clear about your beliefs and wants these areas:

A. You are not satisfied with his/her current level of performance.

B. The performance needs to improve to a level that is satisfactory.

C. Your wish to do all you can to have the employee succeed.

D. If performance does not improve by a specified date, then you will apply consequences (the consequences must be within the boundaries that you can actually do and you must do them or your workers will never trust that you really will follow though).

E. You are clear that "it takes two to tango" and that you play a role in the performance issue. Therefore you are getting help to be as clear as possible and have met with a third party to clarify your expectations of him/her to be as behaviorally specific as possible.

F. You also need help to understand your part in the low performance. Therefore, your employee must also meet with the third party to help them get as clear as possible about what they need from you to be successful.

III. Employee prepares for meeting: Have your employee meet with the third party. Their task is to create a list about what additional ways they need to be managed in order to succeed. To generate the list have them answer this question "in order for me to be successful I need "X" from my boss?"

A. Employee generates their list

B. Third party helps convert each item generated on the list into behavioral specifics.

IV. Troubled employee meeting: Meet with your employee and the neutral third party to share both lists.

A. Make clear your expectations.

B. Get clear of the employee's requests of you.

C. Make appropriate commitments. End with agreements for changed behavior stated in specific terms.

With bosses and employees, this is not an equal among equals conversation. The boss may insist on items that the employee might not be happy about, but of course, the more collaboration in the agreements the better.

Warning – If the third party is neutral but also another high level member of management the employee could have a hard time opening up because of the power imbalance in the room.

V. Follow Through: It is essential to create a plan for effective follow through of the work. There are three types of follow through: Formal, Ongoing, and Long term. To be successful a comprehensive strategy incorporating all forms of follow through must be taken.

A. Formal Follow Up: Have two formal follow up meetings, like outlined below, at a minimum. Base this on the severity, duration, and intensity of the problem. If very severe, the follow up must happen weekly for a few weeks. If mild, then less frequently.
  1. First meeting: Two weeks later meet for the first formal follow up, a "throw-away" evaluation. Note both success and failure and re-clarify expectations and commitments.
  2. Second meeting: Again, two weeks later meet for the second formal follow up. No "throw-away" this time. By now, the dye will be cast. You will know. Nine times out of ten the employee will be succeeding. One in ten, in my experience, will not.
     a. Process for the follow up meetings:
        i. Go through the list of agreements and rate each - are the commitments being followed, and are you getting the intended results? Make adjustments and changes where necessary.
        ii. Ask if any other issues have surfaced and set up new agreements if needed.
        iii. Make plans for the second and third follow up
B. Ongoing: Pay attention on a day to day basis that you are upholding the commitments made during the meeting. Waiting until formal follow up will not do.
C. Long Term: From time to time have a meeting to check in around what's working or not working and what could happen differently to ensure success.

A note about follow up - If you do a good process and skimp on the follow up do not blame the employee for failing. Also, if the relationship has been highly contentious and the problems lingered for years, then you need to have more follow ups. After this consistently reinforce the commitments and agreements made. That includes reinforcing successes with positive informal feedback, instantaneously addressing any relational "pinches" that arise, and taking fast action to try different solutions on any failed efforts.

Paradoxically, if the result of your clearly stated expectations and direct, clear communication with the employee leads to the turn-around, I predict that the problem was not a troubled employee but a troubled relationship. It may also be a systems problem. Look for other employees who lack the clarity they need from you.

P.S. I developed this with the clear intention to greatly reduce undesirable work practices leading to the firing of employees who could have succeeded if a systems change or management clarity about goals had been initiated. I'm proud of those results. However, some of my union colleagues remind me that these steps, in the hands of a manipulative, non-authentic boss, could be used to justify the firing of someone rather than towards helping them succeed. I shudder. They are right. All methods may be used for good or ill.[66]

Third Party Conflict Resolution [67]

by Chris Crosby

All organizational cultures have some amount of conflict. Whereas Appendix K focused on trouble between a boss and employee, this appendix focuses on tension between employees (and departments) that have no authority over each other. Shifting a culture towards managing conflicts constructively and in a direct and problem solving way is part of your responsibility as a leader.

System health is increased by the effective use of third party facilitation to manage conflict. A skilled facilitator[68] will help you to work through the issues, highlight inadvertent systemic pinch points, and create solutions that help the individuals and/or departments in conflict as well as the whole system.

The following third party intervention outline has shown consistent results.

I. Systemic set up for successful outcome: Build appropriate sponsorship for the conflict resolution. Meet with the boss(s) of the employees and first clarify that they expect the employees to improve their working relationship. After that is clear do the following:

    A. Coach the boss to say the following things (the boss IS the sponsor or as Crosby outlines in "Walking the Empowerment Tightrope" the sustaining sponsor).

        1. Tell each employee that they don't have to like each other, but they do have to work well together.

        2. That he/she is using a consultant to work through the problems.

3. If they do not succeed these are the likely consequences (just like with the "Troubled Employee" intervention the consequences must be real).

4. If there are specific tasks or problems that must be handled more constructively, the boss must outline them.

If the boss of either employee does not care whether or not the conflict is resolved, do not go forward. It is a set up to believe that people should "just get along like adults" when the system is clearly not wanting them to. (ie. If either boss does not want this work done, then that employee most often will stay loyal to that request)

II. Interviews: (Prior to each interview, confirm that the sponsor has talked to each employee, set the expectations for the conflict resolution, and has informed them that you will be the third party.) Meet individually with each party to the conflict. Include the following interview components (Do step A, B1 and B2 in order and then the rest of the meeting can be more circular):

A. Confirm that they have talked with the sponsor and verify the message. If the conversation has not happened stop immediately and get the sponsor involved.

B. Explain your role as a facilitator

1. Clarify that you are going to lead the intervention process.

2. Emphasize that you are not going to be an arbitrator and resolve the issue for the parties.

3. State that you are going to, to the degree possible, balance the power among the individuals in the conflict, e.g., between an hourly employee and a department supervisor.

4. Explain that you are going to help the parties reach agreements with "by-when" dates.

5. Clarify that there will be follow-up sessions to make sure that the agreements are being implemented by both parties making commitments.
6. Emphasize that the focus will be on future behavior, not on attempts to determine who was right or wrong in the past.

C. Allow the individual to ventilate his/her feelings and judgments. During the original venting coach for concreteness by helping each employee change their general statements (judgments/inferences) into behavioral specifics.

1. Each time you help them get to the behavioral specific tell them "when we meet with X (the person they are in conflict with), I want you to say the specifics versus those general words.
2. Coach them to say their emotions in a non-blaming way. Spend as much time as necessary in this step and only move to the meeting with both parties in the room if you think the participants are able to say things in a non-blaming and specific way.

D. Get a verbal commitment that they are committed to improving the work relationship with the other individual.

E. Encourage the individual to be specific about his/her problems with the other party. What, where, how, when, and why.

F. Take minimal notes. Remind the individual that you are warming him/her up so that s/he can bring up his/her own issues during the interaction with the other. If however, the participant brings up critical systemic issues that you think must be addressed, contract with them to remind them if during the conversation they forget to bring it up. Then write it down so you remember. (Memory is rarely perfect for anyone)

G. Get permission from the individual to remind him/her during the interaction meeting about issues that s/he brings up during the interview.

III. Third Party Meeting: Bring the parties together to work through the conflict. Each party will take turns working through their issues. (Approximately a two hour meeting).

  A. Opening

    1. Explain the role of the facilitator again.

    2. Get a recommitment from them individually (in front of the other party) that each is committed to improving the work relationship.

  B. Interaction between parties

    1. Process steps for effective interaction. Note: Although these are presented in a sequence, once the dialog starts, it will likely be a circular interaction that moves from step to step freely.

    a. Ventilation: Allow the individuals to share their frustrations. Empathy from you, the third party, without taking sides is the key skill needed in this step. Hopefully, prepared by the interview, the parties are ready to "vent" in a minimally blaming way.

    b. Listen: While the first person is venting the other participants' job is to listen and say back what the person said. No arguing or defending is allowed at this stage. John Wallen states that most conflict happens as a result of the interpersonal gap[69]. Parroting (or as loose version of it) is one way to ensure that people actually heard what the other is saying versus just fighting against it. Forcing listening here slows down the conversation and lessons the intensity. Often when participants parrot accurately, they hear the other for the first time. Almost always it will shift the conflict in a positive direction.

c. Openness: Is about being open to look at your part of the conflict, your emotional reaction to events, and your behavior. Help the individuals move from venting to sharing responsibility for the problem. The components of openness include describing feelings about specific behaviors (by either participants) and each individual being open to learn about how s/he co-created the conflict. Owning is about describing ones part in the co-creation. Owning is not about taking complete responsibility for the entire conflict (i.e. letting the other off the hook) nor is it about explaining or making excuses by telling a story about your past. (Appropriately owning your part of the conflict eases tension yet may better follow step d.)

d. Moccasins: Help each party to walk in the other's moccasins, to understand where the other person is coming from and be able to say "I can see how you could have felt this way."

e. Plan for change

   i. Be specific with examples of the problem.

   ii. Be specific with requests for change.

   iii. Make sure that the requested changes are measurable in some objective way. (A note about what is measurable: Many don't want to write down behavioral items but they must be tracked. Things such as, "If I think you are ignoring a request from me, I will ask". With a simple check this can be tracked.)

   iv. Reciprocity – This means taking appropriate responsibility for my own requests. An example of an inappropriate commitment would be, "OK, I will give you the data when you need it"(when the data is needed at inconsistent times that only the person who needs it knows), versus, "If I want data I will ask" (appropriate reciprocity by the user of the data!). Reciprocity helps the person take appropriate responsibility for their actions versus trying to mind read.

C. Closing
1. Make clear that each party is responsible for keeping track of their own agreements, plus that a written copy of the agreements will go to each boss.
2. Set a time and date for the first follow-up meeting — within one week if the problem is critical

IV. **Follow through:** As with all new adventures follow through is critical. Follow up must happen in a few ways.

A. Informal
1. Share the commitments made in the meeting immediately with the bosses (sponsors) to help them gain clarity and understanding. This can be done alone or, preferably, with their party(s) in the conflict.
2. Highlight any systemic way in which the boss added to the conflict. Systemic issues like role confusion, competing expectations, or lack of decision clarity are common in interpersonal or intergroup conflicts.
3. Finally, coach the boss to monitor the commitments until they are clear that the conflict is resolved.

B. Formal
1. Have at least two follow up meetings. Base this on the severity, duration, and intensity of the conflict. If very severe, the follow up must happen weekly for a few weeks. If mild, then less frequently.

2. Process for the follow up meetings
    a. Go through the list of agreements and rate each - are the commitments being followed, and are you getting the intended results? Make adjustments and changes where necessary.
    b. Ask if any other issues have surfaced and set up new agreements if needed.
    c. Make plans for the second and third follow up meetings.

A NOTE ABOUT SECOND ORDER CHANGE

Throughout the above work, focus on both the immediate agreements (first order change) and the patterns between the two individuals (second order change). Do the latter by insisting that the individuals speak to each other directly—not through you. The goal is that long after the original agreements have been achieved, the two individuals interact with each other in a new pattern enabling them to solve new problems as they arise or even prevent potential problems.[70]

Cultural Change in Organizations

A Guide to (Often) Missing Components of Successful Software Implementation [71]

by Chris Crosby

Most businesses use some form of an Enterprise Resource Planning (ERP) system. Many have a terrible time during initial implementation or subsequent upgrades. Despite this, ERP systems are here to stay. ERP systems (such as Oracle, MAS90, and SAP) are the information systems used to take, manufacture, ship, and account for customer orders, as well as to manage finance, purchasing, sales, planning, and inventory. Once you convert to an ERP system, upgrades and transitions to new systems become a fact of life.

Miss-managed implementations can temporarily cripple operations, cause sharp spikes in workload and stress, and negatively impact the bottom line in a manner far greater than the projected project costs. Research, such as the Standish Report on Project Success, indicates that most implementations go poorly. In fact, only 34% finish on time and within budget, while the rest are either abandoned in midstream (15%), or incur cost and schedule overruns or missing functionality (51%).

The ideas below are not a prescription for all implementations but rather a set of critical levers that may apply to your situation. *The list only includes items that I think are often missing or done in a haphazard way.* Apply them to your situation and decide which levers to pull for your implementation to be as successful as possible.

Obtain support from the top but build support throughout the system – The top leader in your organization must make it clear to everyone that you are implementing a new system and set the expectation that the success or failure is dependent on the whole organization, NOT just the project team.

Set the scope to minimize the impact on the manufacturing floor – Many businesses have multiple systems from different vendors. Each ERP implementation project must choose which old systems get replaced or interfaced into the new system. The process of building appropriate scope should be discussed with key managers with as much clarity as possible as to the risks and benefits to each decision. To the extent possible the manufacturing floor systems should be kept intact unless a clear advantage is shown in replacing the existing systems. If you disrupt the floor, the pain to the customer, and thus to your bottom line, can be immense. The Business Unit I worked for retained our floor system; other BU's did not and paid a tremendous price for it in the form of missed deliveries and disgruntled employees.

Don't sell it once it's bought – Tell the end users with as much clarity as possible what you think they will gain and lose as a result of the software systems. Do not sugarcoat anything. Be honest about how difficult the implementation will be and the amount of work it will require. Most end users have been through system changes before and know that it can be very difficult. If you are upfront with them they will respect you more in the end. On the other hand, if you only point out the great things the system will do while ignoring the constraints, potential problems, and amount of work, you will not only build resistance to the new system but potentially damage your credibility.

Spend time educating the managers above the people who will use the system – The project manager must spend significant time educating key managers on the project. Keep them informed regarding next steps in the time line, project issues, potential problems, key decisions that must be made, and, perhaps most importantly, ongoing resource needs.

Involve the real end users – When configuring the system make sure you involve the people who will do the work, NOT merely a representative. These end users must be your top players and be able to point out any potential issue that will hurt the business. Issues can be solved if raised, but if they are never raised until you start using the system you will be in serious trouble. IT People often say, "Just turn the system on, then we will stabilize it." Do not listen to this logic; it will cause you way more pain than it's worth. Instead, involve the end users in each step of the way.

During each CSI implementation the end users raised on average over 500 issues through the testing process. Each "Go Live" still had a few surprises, but imagine how many we would have had if they had only raised 50.

Cultivate input – During software configuration the goal is to get as much input as possible. When end users raise issues, listen, paraphrase, and write them down. If you can add a "thanks," that is even better. The number one factor on how much input you will generate is how you receive it when it starts coming. After you are clear about the issue they raise, then have a predetermined process to determine whether, and/or how, and when it will be solved. That process must be clear to all participants and continue to be taught, refined and clarified as the project progresses.

Clarify what can be changed and what has to be lived with – Another key to input from your end users is to clarify what has to be adopted and what can be adapted. Don't expect this to be a one time easy conversation. Software systems are complex. The average person will not be able to grasp all the information immediately, and some will push the same issues several times until they really understand it. And well they should because frequently, when pushed, the project team can create solutions that they didn't initially envision, and solve problems that they didn't think they could solve.

The configuration process is a game in which there are several levers that can be pulled, thousands perhaps, and each lever leads to another set of potential solutions and problems. The project team has a full time job to educate the end users helping in the configuration process. This education must be done with patience and grace. The key to good involvement is to set boundaries while rewarding feedback.

Be aware of the trade off between better data for the organization, and more work for end users – Better information does not come free. In all systems anything that you want to obtain at the back end must be input into the system by an end user. In our business the financial people wanted information on the product by piece. A reasonable request, but that information is not used by anyone else in the organization to make better business decisions, and it would have cost an extra man hour per shift to input (as determined through a time study). Getting this data would have cost thousands and given very little in return. Make sure you have a decision process in place that helps sort through the validity of asking for additional input and balances that with basic operation needs.

Have the right and enough technical resources – ERP systems are at best well constructed software programs that are robust and flexible. At worst they are poorly written pieces of software that break down more than operate. Each have series of modules specific to the different business areas such as planning and finance. Many have new modules to meet an ever expanding list of requirements and are filled with bugs and complexities. Expect to spend a lot of money on technical resources to assist with the more complex or newer modules, or to suffer the consequences if you don't. Slow progress in getting modules up to speed could signal the wrong, or most likely, insufficient technical resources. With technical resources, you truly pay now or pay later.

Create clarity of decision making, especially when it comes to moving from testing to using the system – Most software implementation projects proceed in stages from configuration to testing, and finally "go-live." At each stage, *there should be a decision making process which balances influence from the end users* who are helping to configure the system. Including the end users creates a decision matrix between the BU lead team, the local lead team, the end users, and the project team. Do not allow the project team to make decision recommendations to the BU and location lead team without the voice of the end users.

During our implementations, at the end of each stage, end users from each area impacted by the project raised their critical issues to the local lead team. They also indicated if their area was ready to move forward to the next stage or should take a "time-out" and solve critical issues. The local lead team weighed the information in terms of overall impact to the location and made their suggestion to the BU lead team who in turn made the final decision. The project team *facilitated* the process, along with adding their opinions.

The above process caused several things to happen. First, we did not go live on a few occasions as planned. Second, the end users and the location lead team were significantly informed of each issue at risk. Finally, when we did go live the end users were ready and in most cases, were actually lobbying to turn the system on.

Do not skimp on go live support – Most people understand that there is a difference between classroom training and working in a live system. Make sure you have enough support to help anybody with keystroke needs for the first few weeks after go-live, and do not leave until the end users and the internal location person say it's ok.

This guide is intended to help prep and plan your ERP system adventure. I cannot say this enough: to be most effective, besides choosing the right system, you must plan all facets of your implementation.

Every ERP system, like every business and every location, is different. Each has its own problems that must be solved to achieve an effective implementation. Your needs will be dictated by your unique situation. I have seen ERP implementations where no added technical expertise was needed, for instance, but I have also seen projects suffer because the right help was obtained only after a delay.

Software implementations can go smoother than the industry norm. The implementation within Alcoa CSI certainly did. This guide covers the pieces missing or miss-managed in most implementations. May it serve you well in your future ERP adventures.

Cultural Change in Organizations

A Breakthrough Technology for Achieving Rapid Results in Projects, Initiatives, and R&D[72]

TURNAROUND INTENSIVE PLANNING INTERVENTION™

Achieving successful project execution, major initiatives, or product development outcomes when such undertakings are in serious trouble is an art form. To do so requires the integration of both technical and (often missing) human-dimension factors. This article focuses on how to complete – on schedule and within budget – key projects as well as how to redirect projects at midpoint to recover lost time and money.

WHAT LEVEL OF RESULTS CAN BE EXPECTED?

Example: A two-and-a-half day planning session, utilizing the Turnaround Intensive Planning Intervention™ (TIPI), was held in a Fortune 500 manufacturing company where production delays were jeopardizing the firm's contract with another Fortune 500 company. Within 90 days the project team had exceeded its goal, more than doubling its previous output, and in another 30 days, production was increased by another 15 percent. By the sixth month, the firm had more than tripled production and, in one day, actually quadrupled the original output. This translates into a daily production increase from 600 products per day to 2000 per day. Throughout the process, the team maintained quality control.

Example: In a manufacturing plant in Badin, North Carolina, as reported in the Associated Press in the mid 90's, the county's largest employer was threatening to close if cost reductions of $5.5 million could not be achieved. Six months after implementing TIPI in the plant and working to identify areas for reducing costs, the plant was able to confidently project a budget far exceeding that goal.

Example: A nuclear utility experiencing a prolonged outage was seriously behind schedule on a complex project to refurbish motor operated valves. The project involved personnel from almost every department in the utility (e.g., Production, Maintenance, Purchasing, Engineering, Materials Receipt, and so forth). The plant was losing $1 million a day and could not reopen unless the project was completed. The project was six months behind schedule, and none of the required 150 valves had been completed. After TIPI intervention, all components were completed four months ahead of the original target date.

GENERAL CHARACTERISTICS OF THE TURNAROUND INTENSIVE PLANNING INTERVENTION™ PROCESS

The eight essential principles for success underlying these impressive results include the following:

1. Failure or potential failure must be openly recognized by nearly all those who are involved in the project.
2. The consequences of such failure must be clearly accepted as costly to the organization and, potentially, to the individuals involved.
3. Conversely, a positive payoff for success must be evident. If schedule delays are standard practice and no consequences have been apparent to involved employees, then the TIPI will not work. In that case, the plant manager must make clear both negative and/or positive consequences of failure or success.
4. The key sponsoring manager must initiate this intervention and must assure that each boss of any participant is also positively sponsoring the intervention.

5. Knowledgeable employees must be involved in the process – every engineer, mechanic, software programmer, purchaser and so forth.

In the nuclear utility intervention referenced earlier, 21 first-line supervisors were present on the first day. Only one had worked closely enough to the project to contribute knowledge to the intensive planning activity. The other 20 said that they were there to learn but knew little about the day-to-day, nitty-gritty of the project. Within 45 minutes, however, the facilitator obtained from them a list of 42 additional personnel who needed to be present if the intervention was to succeed. The meeting was dismissed until the next day when the supervisors, most of their bosses, and the 42 personnel were present for a kick-off session. Introducing the session, the key manager explained his goals for the intervention. He explained why he had made the decision to intervene in this way and made clear his expectation that members set aside their daily "crisis" activities, and give their full attention to the work of planning a successful turnaround. As if they were in a major sporting game, the team was pausing at half time to assess why they were losing, how they could win, and what new tactics would be needed. To do this, all the players had to be present.

With the new members present, the facilitator encouraged participants to identify additional key workers who were missing. After a few phone calls, these participants quickly appeared.

Of course, it is rarely feasible to have all knowledgeable employees present. While some missing employees may also hold critical information, the process described in this article has been successful as long as those who are present have broad experience and knowledge of the daily challenges, including process breakdowns, equipment dilemmas and so forth and have an open communication channel with those who are absent.

6. There is a definable list of qualities that help in facilitating the process. The facilitator needs to be:

♦ Neutral about issues. A facilitator can best be neutral when s/he comes from a "not-knowing" position. Not knowing the inside jargon and the technical aspects of the project heightens the facilitator's awareness of the continual need for clarity.

♦ Capable of asserting personal authority, both in moving the process and in guiding conflict resolution.

♦ Clear about his/her role as facilitator, which includes personal clarity that s/he is not present to be the sponsor, nor the advocate of substantive ideas, nor the project manager. In short, this is not the facilitator's project. S/he does not have to, and should not, convince others of its importance. That's the sponsor's job, including especially the sustaining sponsors (that is, the immediate boss of each participant).

♦ Clear about the problem-solving steps crucial to this intervention. This includes being capable of organizing a large group of participants and managing a multi-step process to identify the critical issues blocking success and to plan wisely to resolve these issues.

♦ Highly skilled in his/her ability to achieve clarity in the project.

7. The process must aim problem-solving at key issues or themes and fully integrate socio-technical insights to both create and sustain the critical changes developed in the sessions.

8. The Project Manager must have the capability to manage the agreed-upon schedule, commitments and decision-authority matrix, without becoming either authoritarian or succumbing to permissive extremes that often are disguised and encouraged as "consensus."

WHAT IS "SOCIO-TECHNICAL"?

The "socio" aspects include everything about a project (or product development or a manufacturing process, etc.) that are not technical. These may be classified as intrapersonal, interpersonal, group, or systemic factors. The TIPI intervention program focuses on systemic change and management factors including a strong emphasis on technical issues.

WHAT DOES A "SYSTEMIC ISSUE" LOOK LIKE?

PageMaker 5.0, the original desktop software, was nearly a year late when it was released in the early 1990's. Since the project represented nearly 50% of the company's revenue, this had been a serious delay.

A major systemic issue in the production of version 5.0 was the lack of decision-making accountability in connection with 20 key issues. Since software product development is a highly matrixed process (across almost all departments), the "stuck" decision-making points were a major factor causing delays.

By contrast, in the PageMaker 6.0 project, these 20 factors were identified and a single individual was named who would make necessary decisions in a timely manner when an impasse was reached. As a result of this and other changes, PageMaker 6.0 was produced on time.

In the multi-billion dollar project for the Department of Energy, Crosby & Associates consulted with Los Alamos National Laboratories and, according to the project director, "...helped to establish a single point of accountability and to develop open lines of communication within the organization. Crosby's techniques helped to identify and resolve many 'stuck' decision-making points.[73]"

WHAT ABOUT INTRAPERSONAL, INTERPERSONAL AND GROUP FACTORS?

Skilled facilitators are present during the planning intervention to help participants avoid unproductive conflicts and dysfunctional behavior. The facilitators help participants to utilize differences in productive ways, that is, to deal with different points of view directly by being specific (not general and theoretical) and non-blaming and by listening so as to understand the other's point of view. *The facilitators are not present to teach these skills!* Such skills can be learned but not during the intervention process simply because the learning of these skills takes a longer time and a different process. It is important to note, however, that what we call "personality problems" in teams often mask underlying interpersonal, group process or systemic issues.

COMPONENTS OF A SUCCESSFUL PLANNING INTERVENTION

The TIPI process is a custom intervention that normally lasts three days and should include the following components:

- The Initiating Sponsor (single point leader over all in the session) makes a statement including specific measurable goals, the final completion date, and a prediction about the consequences of success or failure.
- The most experienced employees, who actually do the tasks, must be present.
- The room is divided into critical areas or themes for a working session.
- The project manager who will guide the follow up is introduced. Their role is made clear, especially that they are NOT the boss. Rather, they track and report what is or is not happening. Also tracked is what's 2-4 weeks ahead to assure that those with single-point accountable will be on schedule.

- A process to identify forces that may impede success is begun in the groups.
- A process to identify solutions to the above forces follows.
- Each solution has an SPA as well as a completion date identified.
- Each group creates a timeline of tasks.
- Each timeline gets integrated to a master timeline.
- Organizational theory of Sponsor/Agent/Target/ Advocate is taught to all and each group charts their members and highlights potential pinch points.
- Decision clarity is created for each potential tough issue, based on the unique history that workers have. Then the right people are put on the decision matrix to resolve each issue. (See page 59)
- Follow up and project execution are planned, communicated, and executed.

SUMMARY

This intervention integrates the best technical knowledge (residing in experienced engineers, operators, maintenance personnel, and other craftspersons) and systemic "socio" factors that are typically missing in traditional project management and product development undertakings. Interpersonal factors must be managed here as in any team process. However, many so-called interpersonal problems or personality conflicts stem from these systemic and socio factors being overlooked in routine project operations. When these considerations are overlooked, projects go awry. In this intervention, technical problems are addressed since the best, most knowledgeable technicians are involved. But neither technical nor even interpersonal problems are the primary culprit in most product or production delays. Rather, it's the lack of understanding and strategy about systemic socio factors. This TIPI process makes up for that lack of understanding and strategy resulting in a time-line to be managed that includes the key strategic elements usually missing. Cultural elements such as clarity about decision making, accountability, input from employees without extremes of consensus, and follow-through are strengthened.

Footnote text

1 Published by HRD Quarterly, King of Prussia, PA, 1992.
2 Published by Vivo! Publishing Co., Inc., Seattle, WA, 2011.
3 Friedman, Edwin. *Generation to Generation: Family Processes in Church and Synagogue.* Guilford Press, New York, NY. 1985.
4 Organization Development: A Process of Learning and Changing, Second Edition by Dr. W. Warner Burke, Teachers College, Columbia University, Page 9, Addison-Wesley Publishing Company, 1992
5 Thanks to Dr. Tim Weber for this distinction.
6 Greenleaf, Robert. *Servant Leadership.* Paulist Press, New York, NY. 1977, pp. 66 and 24.
7 See Chapter 7, page 83.
8 See Chapter 5, page 63
9 See Appendix D
10 A strategy for an evolutionary rather than revolutionary way to accelerate movement towards less supervision and more autonomy is outlined in Chapters 4 & 5.
11 I credit this to Thomas Gordon, creator of Parent Effectiveness Training.
12 The book *Walking the Empowerment Tightrope: Balancing Management Authority and Employee Influence* by the author (HRD Quarterly, King of Prussia, PA, 1992) is built around 25 High-Performance Factors that were first presented at a NASA Quality Conference following the Challenger disaster. For example, clear sponsorship, single-point accountability, decision clarity, employee influence, and by-when clarity. These or questions chosen from my previous book can be used and quickly scored to begin a problem solving process with intact groups. Also see Appendix D for a culture shift questionnaire that has been used with great success.
13 The survey, *The People Performance Profile*, was developed by Robert P. Crosby and John Scherer.
14 This is sometimes called a "360 process" where data is gathered from one's boss, peers, and employees. This process can be redeemed if anonymous evaluations are screened so that they reflect descriptions of behavior rather than accusations and if the recipient has an opportunity for live dialogue with evaluators in a non-blaming, supportive, problem-solving way, such as illustrated in Chapter 6. The more skills employees and managers have, the more they can abandon anonymous feedback.
15 See Chapter 6 for the blow-by-blow account and information on conflict resolution processes.
16 This process is described in Chapters 4 and 5.
17 From consulting work done by David Crosby.
18 See Factor 25, Chapter 3 of *Walking the Empowerment Tightrope: Balancing Management Authority and Employee Influence* for ideas about breaking up such dysfunctional behavior.

[19] From *Solving the Cross-Work Puzzle: Succeeding in the Modern Organization* by the author (Vivo! Publishing, Seattle, WA, 2010, p 11).

[20] The activities outlined here are contained in a training program for managers and supervisors called *ToughStuff™*. (Naming it is inconsistent with the author's recommendations mentioned elsewhere in this book. People will call it something—perhaps "Leadership" is sufficient.) Such training is available bi-yearly through Crosby & Associates (www.crosbyod.com or See page iv contact info). It is also called "Emotional Intelligence at Work" and is open to all who want to improve their skills. Crosby & Associates also hold Tough Stuff trainings internally in locations throughout the globe which adds the greatest gain because the leader and their employees raise the overall skill level of the organization together. Caution: It is my belief that implementing any training methodology without an overall organizational strategy tied to business objectives, such as Peter develops in the first pages of Chapter 1, will have minimal impact.

[21] See Chapter 6.

[22] Don Simonic invented this ingenious process. He formerly managed the ALCOA Addy (Washington) Magnesium Plant (Northwest Alloys) and the Tennessee and Warrick, Indiana ALCOA Aluminum Plants (simultaneously!). It was after his tenure at Northwest Alloys that *Business Week* claimed a "72% productivity gain" (June, 1992). He had just begun at the Tennessee plant when the selection for training example occurred. The significance that he placed on the training outlined on pages 29, 30 and 32 supplemented by all that is contained in this book is even more apparent when one realizes that he was selecting participants for a 12-week (over two years) corporate master's program!

[23] In January, 1995, Volvo announced plans to reopen the Uddevalla plant in a joint venture with TWR Ltd., (Oxfordshire, England) with TWR owning 51% of the new business.

[24] Gleckman, Howard. "The Technology Payoff," *Business Week*, June 14, 1993, pp. 56-68.

[25] *Metals Week*, November ,1992.

[26] Adler, P. and Cole, R. "Designed for Learning: A Tale of Auto Plants," *Sloan Management Review*, Spring, 1993, pp. 85-94, and Berggren, C. "NUMMI vs. Uddevalla," *Sloan Management Review*, Winter, 1994, pp. 37-46.

[27] These are illustrated in Chapters 1-3. See the goal graph in Chapter 1.

[28] Addy was one of only two magnesium plants in the United States. China, Russia, and Israel were eventually able to sell in the U.S. at a lower price because of less expensive labor, materials, and power. The Addy Plant could not match the price and was forced to close in 2001. This was in spite of the outstanding leadership of the manager Jerry Turnbow and the continued record-setting performances by motivated and skilled employees.

[29] Adapted from *Walking the Empowerment Tightrope: Balancing Management Authority and Employee Influence.*

[30] Bennis, Warren. *Why Leaders Can't Lead.* Jossey-Bass, San Francisco, CA. 1989, pp. 27 and 61.

[31] Dewey, John. *Experience and Education.* Macmillan Publishing Company, New York, NY. 1938. This landmark work contains his critique of both traditional and progressive education.

Footnotes

32 See Chapter 3, Factor 3 on "Influence" in *Walking the Empowerment Tightrope: Balancing Management Authority and Employee Influence*, p. 26.

33 Joel Baker, first-line supervisor, inspired this "Howard" story.

34 One can only sponsor direct reports. Even the CEO's sponsorship is limited to his/her direct reports and his/her capability to help them build sponsorship (therefore alignment) with their direct reports. Championing a cause is possible but minimally effective. For effective change that will be sustained, sponsorship is critical and more difficult than "championing" (which is how the word *sponsorship* is usually used) but the only enduring way to go. Anything short of on-going sponsorship/leadership as defined here will create a spawning ground for one fad after another. (See the article on fads in the Appendix and reread p. 27 & 28.) But let's go back to the CEO. Of course the CEO carries a lot of weight in the organization and can begin or endorse all major changes that impact the entire workplace. But they must understand the realities of their authority below their direct reports. They have referent (who you know), technical (what you know), and interpersonal (how well you interact) power everywhere. But the CEO, like any boss at any level, drives changes by holding their direct reports accountable to the appropriate behaviors that will continue to drive the change, and in turn their direct reports must do the same and so on until the whole organization is aligned. If you skip layers when driving change then the layers will inadvertently cause the change to fail.

35 Doing this with one's direct reports can be a very effective change activity.

36 From *Solving The Cross-Work Puzzle: Succeeding in the Modern Organization*, p. 54.

37 This is what inspired Peter to do the *ToughStuff*™ training in Chapter 3. What's required to lead is not simply a philosophical change. Would that it were. Rather, what's required is attitudinal and behavioral change. *ToughStuff*™ is designed to do this as well as train employees to be aware of systemic issues.

38 Until late 1996, Don Simonic managed two major ALCOA plants, one in Tennessee and one in Indiana. Obviously, it takes masterly delegation and monitoring skills to do this. These plants have achieved world-class performance in many dimensions.

39 The survey instrument *The People Performance Profile* used in over 600 companies reveals that about 25-30% of all employer-employee work relationships are in crisis such as illustrated in this chapter. Unless those dysfunctional work relationships are changed, other initiatives (autonomy, re-engineering, and so forth) have minimal chance of success.

40 See the short story entitled *From Victim to Creator* for a tale about how an hourly employee becomes such a facilitator. Hourly facilitators help not just non-salaried workers but supervisors and other salaried employees as well.

41 In "FIGHT, FLIGHT, FREEZE - Taming Your Reptilian Brain and Other Practical Approaches to Self Improvement," by Gilmore Crosby, Eloquent Books, New York, NY, 2008, the author includes a "Specificity Quiz" designed to aid in distinguishing facts from interpretations, an exceedingly difficult and important skill.

42 See Appendix L for an outline on third-party consultation.

43 In a survey of 713 companies, 26% who downsized from 1992-94 reported higher productively after downsizing and 24% reported a decline. 86% of all downsizing firms reported a negative impact on employee morale. (American Management Association, 1994 survey).

44 Thanks to Rob Schachter for this illustration.

45 See "Succeeding With Troubled Employees" in Appendix K.

46 Ross Snyder, who taught at the Chicago Theological Seminary from 1941 until about 1977, inspired that work. He and his student Ruth Emory deserve credit for this important focus.

47 Ruth Emory, "A Point of View for Participating in a Ministry With Youth," mimeographed (1960). Reprinted with the author's permission.

48 Adapted from *Living With Purpose When The Gods Are Gone* by the author. Times Change Press, Ojai, CA. 1991.

49 Greenleaf, Robert. *Ibid*, p. 7.

50 Osbon, Diane K, Editor. *A Joseph Campbell Companion*. Harper Collins, New York, NY. 1991, p. 175.

51 These astonishing decreases are not a fantasy but rather the actual experience of an organization.

52 The *ToughStuff*™ training that this supervisor participated in is described on pages 29 and 30, also see footnote 20.

53 Adapted from the supervisory work of George Chapman.

54 Thanks to Michael Heinrich for his editing work on this piece.

55 A team of independent high-performance experts interviewed many of the employees from both of the companies referenced here and obtained much anecdotal data as to how the change strategy contributed to increases in productivity and quality.

56 This process was created in collaboration with Jeff Reynolds while working at the Alcoa plant in Fusina, Italy.

57 Lessons from the PECO Nuclear turnaround – both a strong nuclear safety and a high productivity culture are built on the same behavioral foundations, and can be reliably implemented and sustained. This article first appeared in an edition of *Human Factors: Special Edition - Volume 7, Issue SE*. Human Factors is our free tri-yearly newsletter that you can sign up for on our website www.crosbyod.com.

58 Conner, D. R. (1992). *Managing at The Speed of Change*. New York: Random House, Inc.

59 Crosby, R. P. (1992). *Walking the Empowerment Tightrope*. King of Prussia, PA: Organization Design and Development, Inc.

60 Crosby, R. P. (1994). *Solving the Cross-Work Puzzle*. Seattle: Vivo! Publishing Co., Inc., re-released in 2010.

61 Dr. Ronald Lippitt and Dr. Charles Jung developed the model from which this article is derived. Their model describes the distinction between knowledge retrieval and implication derivation. Following guidelines such as are in Appendix I, a staff or consultant expert will build a collaborative relationship with those who are to use the expert's knowledge. When that happens, advice and even recommendations will be welcomed. (Jung, C., & Lippitt, R. Study of Change as a Concept in Research Utilization. *Theory into Practice*. Feb. 1966, 5(1) 25-29. Published by the College of Education, Ohio State University.)

Footnotes

62 This article first appeared in an edition of *Human Factors: Global Edition – Volume 2, Issue 1*. Human Factors is our free tri-yearly newsletter that you can sign up for on our website www.crosbyod.com.

63 Adapted from *Walking the Empowerment Tightrope* by the author, p. 91.

64 Behavioral specifics is one of the four key John Wallen skills associated with the interpersonal gap. Wallen claims this is the hardest of all skills and the one that gets more difficult when anxious.

65 The following is a list of third party facilitator qualities necessary for effective work. Adapted from MANAGING CONFLICT: Interpersonal Dialogue and Third-Party Roles, Addison-Wesley Publishing Company, Inc. by Richard E. Walton.
 1. High expertise in process work
 2. Low power over the fate participants
 3. High control over process
 4. Moderate knowledge of issues involved
 5. Third party neutrality
 See also page 192.

66 Thanks to Dan Lampton and many other students in the 1998 Corporate Masters Program for their feedback, concerns, and help which is especially reflected in the P.S. on page 174

67 The original outline for this appendix was developed by Patricia Crosby. Special thanks to Richard E. Walton who first introduced me to 'Third Party' work through his original publication of MANAGING CONFLICT: Interpersonal Dialogue and Third-Party Roles, Addison-Wesley Publishing Company, Inc.

68 The following is a list of third party facilitator qualities necessary for effective work. Adapted from MANAGING CONFLICT: Interpersonal Dialogue and Third-Party Roles, Addison-Wesley Publishing Company, Inc. by Richard E. Walton.
 1. High expertise in process work
 2. Low power over the fate participants
 3. High control over process
 4. Moderate knowledge of issues involved
 5. Third party neutrality
 See also page 192.

69 From *Walking the Empowerment Tightrope*, Appendix O, by Robert P. Crosby

70 Third party conflict work is intended to resolve conflicts, raise system awareness, and build skills in each participant. If led well, the conflict will be resolved and systems issues such as role confusion, unclear accountability, and fuzzy decision making will be uncovered and solved. During the process the participants constantly engage with each other primarily rather than just through the third party. Because of this, they do the work of resolving the conflict which helps them build skills and, most importantly, gain the ability and confidence to do the same in the future without the need of a third party.

71 Chris was the Organizational Development Specialist on Alcoa's Closure Systems International (CSI) Oracle implementation (known within Alcoa as the Enterprise Business System or EBS). This appendix

combines wisdom learned from that project, his experience as an OD professional, and a unique adaptation of an effective cultural change strategy.

72 According to William P. Bishop, Defense Programs for the Department of Energy in Washington, D.C., "Not only does Crosby & Associates have a proven and effective process, but they necessarily apply their techniques in new situations with new people. Watching them in such a setting is like watching fine jazz musicians come together for the first time to improvise, with all their tools, a fine new arrangement. Their approach doesn't just work; they make it work."

73 See page 59.

Footnotes